BEYOND
THE
LAW

BEYOND THE LAW

Living the
Sermon on the Mount

Philip K. Clemens

 **Herald Press**

Scottdale, Pennsylvania
Waterloo, Ontario

Library of Congress Cataloging-in-Publication Data

Clemens, Philip K., 1941-
  Beyond the law : living the sermon on the mount / Philip K.
Clemens.
  p. cm.
  Includes bibliographical references.
  ISBN 0-8361-9361-X (pbk. : alk. paper)
  1. Sermon on the mount—Criticism, interpretation, etc.
  2. Christian life. I. Title.
  BT380.3.C54 2007
  226.906—dc22
                                                  2006033234

To order or request information, please call
1-800-759-4447 (individuals); 1-800-245-7894 (trade).
Web site: www.heraldpress.com

To the people of Beaverdam Mennonite Church,
faithful partners in ministry
and rich soil for the seed of the kingdom;

and

to Nancy,
my loving companion these many years,
for her quiet reflection and valued insight

Contents

Foreword

Anyone who attempts a new look at something as thoroughly scrutinized and debated as the Sermon on the Mount is a courageous soul indeed. Philip K. Clemens has done just that, and in so doing has brought fresh light and life to a text that in the Anabaptist tradition has often been termed the "Magna Carta" of the Christian life. As Clemens so effectively argues, the Sermon invites believers in community to embrace a path that transcends the bounds of "do's and don'ts" and internalizes the DNA of God's will and way. It is this intimate embodiment of God that enables the believing community as a whole to express Christ-likeness.

This is an epistle of encouragement and an invitation to the church to live fully into its potential. It offers a word of reprieve for any who have struggled with the impossible call to "be perfect as God is perfect." It provides a clear but gentle scriptural corrective to prevailing individualistic spiritualities by placing the teaching and call of the Sermon on the Mount squarely within the context of the church as community, God's chosen instrument to incarnate the good news of reconciliation, redemption, security and peace in a culture acutely in need of these things.

Beyond the Law offers a helpful reminder of the core values of the Christian faith. Written at a time when both the United States and Canada are actively engaged in war and are increasingly demanding declarations of loyalty from their citizens, Clemens issues a clear call to Christians to pledge their only allegiance to Jesus Christ. In a time when North American culture is more obsessed with security than at any point in its history, this book offers insightful guidance on the nature of security for citizens of the kingdom of God. It includes a very helpful appendix on the Christian call to live as peacemakers in all aspects of life.

The strength of Clemens' writing lies in his ability to bring together sound biblical study with a pastoral heart profoundly rooted in the life of the church he serves. With the aid of an eclectic and excellent assortment of stories, he illustrates the relevance of the Sermon on the Mount for the issues and concerns facing the church and the world today. Thus he seeks throughout to help the reader make practical application of the text to the life of the believing community.

Suitable for use in forming the faith of new believers and in the congregation, this book can help the church rediscover its identity as God's reconciled and reconciling community, and its vocation as God's chosen instrument of blessing for the world. I commend it as a resource that both renews and inspires.

> *Dave Bergen*
> *Executive Secretary for Christian Formation*
> *Mennonite Church Canada*

Preface

The Sermon on the Mount is neither fantasy nor fiction. It is a real-life word from Jesus on how to live. Yet though we believe the Bible to be true, we may take exception when Scripture rubs us the wrong way. We may even think that it's for another age or that it just won't work in our situation.

And we sometimes view the Sermon on the Mount like this: Oh, the Beatitudes are good, if we don't push them too far. We find the Lord's Prayer familiar and soothing. Some of the Sermon's proverbs roll easily off our tongues: "Seek ye first the kingdom of God." "Judge not that ye be not judged." "Do unto others as you would have them do unto you."

But then there's the confusing command to surpass the righteousness of the scribes and Pharisees in order to enter heaven, and the puzzling statement about casting pearls before swine. And what about loving your enemies? How do we take *that*? Although most of us revere this classic Sermon, for whatever reasons, we appear to know very little about its practical application in our everyday lives.

My own regard for the Sermon on the Mount needed revitalization, and 9/11 gave it a jump-start. When America experienced the crushing tragedy of that September morning, we became a wounded country and focused our attention on finding and eliminating the perpetrators of that attack. And we sang, "God Bless America." Meanwhile, Christian voices clashed, and to this day the religious landscape of our country is marred by a widening gulf of partisan loyalties.

13

In such a confusing and troubling situation, basic questions come to mind: Where does our security lie? What is God's kingdom and whom does it include? Do national boundaries and geographical locations relate to the kingdom of Christ? Is there such a thing as a Christian nation? Can legislation make a nation more Christian? Is it appropriate for Christian groups to relate to their home country differently from how they relate to other countries? What is the gospel message?

During the anxious times following 9/11, the text of the Sermon on the Mount took on major proportions for me. Chapters 5 to 7 of Matthew, I discovered, hold answers to all those unsettling questions, and more. But this classic Sermon, that so-called "Manifesto of Christ," appears to be the best-known and least-obeyed teaching of Jesus.[1] Here Jesus teaches how the righteousness of God is designed to pour out from untold riches into the community of faithful believers and to flow through them as blessings into all the world around. How have we been missing that? I asked. How have I been missing it?

I am concerned that often the church's evangelistic witness starts and stops with a message aimed only at the individual, important as that may be. To make a decision for Christ is an individual one, but not private. Just as God created a community of followers by liberating them from slavery in Egypt, so God continues to create a community of followers by liberating them from sin. Salvation is personal, but it is also communal, and that combination creates a far-reaching impact. It was the community to whom Jesus entrusted the making of disciples and their baptism, while teaching them to obey his commands (see Matthew 28:18-20). It was the community to which Jesus said, "A new command I give you: Love one another. As I have loved you, so you must love one another. By this everyone will know that you are my disciples, if you love one another" (John 13:34-35 TNIV).

We cannot love one another if we remain alone, separate from each other. The New Testament is full of teaching on "one-anothering" relationships, and that means community. But because of theological and doctrinal differences, we construct specific definitions for "the Christian" and defend personal and denominational views on what it means to be "born again." We use a kind of scorecard to recognize the good Christian from the bad one. We even believe that because we've said certain words we are "saved."

But after I accept Christ, then what? How does the individual Christian relate to the community of Christ, the fellowship we call church? What are individuals being saved to be and to do? Ron Sider, author and president of Evangelicals for Social Action, says that being saved "is a lot more than just a new right relationship with God through forgiveness of sins. It's a new, transformed lifestyle that you can see visible in the body of believers."[2] Henry Blackaby, pastor and author, agrees:

> I can't tell you how many times I hear Christians crying out for "something more" in their relationship with God. They have accepted Christ into their lives but don't seem to know what to do next. They hear others talking about abundant life in Christ, but abundant life seems to be just beyond their grasp. They become frustrated and depressed, even to the point of desperation. Their struggle tends to come from the fact that they never understood the nature of God's great salvation. More specifically, they never understood the corporate nature of salvation and their significant place within the people of God.[3]

The book you have in your hands is a layperson's guide to discovering how God lives and moves among ordinary people. It is for those who seek to know Christ and to know what it means to follow him in everyday life, whether they have already made that commitment or are pondering it. For everyone, this book is a window through which to see how

God's righteousness is meant to be embodied in our personal and community lives and how the lavish blessings of God give us abundant life as we share those blessings with others. If the gospel message is that Jesus saves us from death and hell for reconciliation with God and each other, then that good news means we are being saved for community in Christ. The first chapter of John offers the ideal evangelistic message: "Come and see!" Come and see the Christ who lives among us (see John 1:39). If we have no vibrant community, our proclamation is empty.

When someone asked award-winning poet Jean Janzen why she writes, she replied with keen insight: "I write so that I know what I'm thinking." I find that true for me too not only in writing this book, but also in my work as a pastor and teacher. The cherished opportunities and demands inherent in pastoral ministry help me to identify and articulate the countless, marvelous things I learn about Bible study and church and about the practical application of the Christian faith.

This book is not an ethics text or a biblical commentary but rather a pastoral meditation that has grown out of my involvement in daily congregational ministry. In the lingering national disquiet after 9/11, Beaverdam Mennonite Church in Corry, Pennsylvania, where I served at that time, became much more than just passively involved. Their enthusiastic collaboration with me in Bible-study classes, sermons, and worship invigorated me. Together we searched the meaning of Jesus' words and pondered their application in our everyday life. I am indebted to those faithful friends and co-workers for the opportunity to preach and teach from Christ's Sermon over a number of months and for the support and encouragement they continuously gave me. Always I was aware that our shared exploration of this beloved Bible passage was not just an academic exercise but a vital activity on which our lives depended. Thank you, my dear friends.

As I focused on this writing project, I was also aware of the thorough and faithful work of scholars, theologians, and pastors who, over the decades and centuries, have preserved and opened the Scriptures for all of us. I am indebted to them for inviting me to the place where I can think and write from within the context of the Christian community. I thank those who have vigorously discussed the concepts of this book with me and have passed along their ideas and encouragement. In particular I thank my faithful colleagues in ministry, Ernest Martin, Wayne Nitzsche, and Robb Esh, for their support and interest. Thanks to editor Michael Degan for his careful and sensitive work, and to the others at Herald Press who detected something of worth in my yet unfinished manuscript. Special thanks go to Nancy, my wife, and to our son, Jim, and his wife, Angie, with their children, Alex and Lena, and to our daughter, Judy, and her husband, Steve, with their children, Tristan and Sophia. Their encouragement has been invaluable. And though they are unaware of it, my grandchildren have taught me a great deal about the wonder of living as children in God's kingdom.

I am thankful that God's Holy Spirit works mightily within the community of the faithful. Certainly the ideas I share in this book are not mine alone but are my shaping of thoughts and convictions according to what has been given so graciously to all of us. I invite you to help me "know what I'm thinking."

—*Philip K. Clemens*

— 1 —

Rules and Righteousness
A Piano Lesson

A woman came to me and asked, "What does your church allow?" Her question caught me off guard, and I found myself at a loss for words. The question was innocent enough, and genuine, but how could I respond to it on her terms without making an issue of it? I knew a bit about her religious background because she had become acquainted with our congregation. Could I tell her that the question was not a good place to start, that "you can't get there from here"? It was not the time or place for us to discuss the question's appropriateness, but I couldn't just deflect it by suggesting that she had an inadequate concept of church, nor would it be polite. I had to come up with something better than that.

I cannot remember what I said, but after stumbling around for a few moments, I came up with something I hoped would be helpful. Later, as I pondered the inquiry, I realized the woman had asked what many people in the Christian church continue to ask: "What am I allowed to do? What rules do I need to follow?" The pages that follow are my answer to that question.

Many people inside and outside the church believe it operates by rules. The church is often viewed as an authority that dispenses lists of do's and don'ts: Read your Bible every day, pray every day, participate in a small group, give ten percent of your money to the church, attend worship at least once a week, do not mow the lawn on Sunday, do not smoke, do not drink, do not swear, do not gamble, wear your hair this way, dress that way, and drive this kind of car.

Strange as it seems, many of us welcome such a list of rules that tells us exactly what to do to be "a good Christian." By checking off the rules as we obey them, we find reassurance as to how we stand before God.

How have we come to this popular misconception of the Christian faith? Do we see "church" the same way we see society around us? Our everyday lives are permeated with lists of rules and regulations. We are saturated with traffic laws, dress codes, real estate stipulations, and the niceties of courtesy and etiquette. Whether we're at home or at work, on the ball field or at church, we're never really free from the dictates of rules. A soccer dad says,

> When my seven-year-old daughter played soccer for the first time, her coach was fantastic. He had the team playing well, winning most of their games primarily because he always reminded the girls to "keep their positions." When other teams were swarming to the ball in clumps of arms and legs, our girls were spaced evenly around the field, passing the ball, defending their territory and making use of the whole field. One game, though, Natalie, a really fine defender, ran up against the limits of the coach's rules. As the ball was coming toward midfield, Natalie ran toward it. But all of a sudden she stopped right at the midfield stripe. No one from the other team was anywhere near the ball, so all the crazed parents yelled, "Go get it, Natalie. Go get the ball." With her toes on the chalk line, she looked over at the sideline, bewildered. "I can't," she said. "I'm not supposed to go past midfield. I need to play my position." Every athletic instinct told Natalie to go get that ball, but her obedience to the coach's instructions would only let her run up to the line. So we all hollered, and watched, as the other team retrieved that loose ball.[1]

A law like driving on the right side of the road becomes so deep-seated that we apply that habit to other parts of our lives, like staying to the right on a sidewalk. Other laws become so pointless or out of date that hardly anyone pays attention to them. One Alabama law says it's illegal to wear a false mustache in church because it might make people laugh. In Indiana, monkeys are forbidden from smoking cigarettes.[2]

Inadequate as laws are, why do we make them? Because the reality of life demands them. If our communities had no rules, we might experience disorder at the least, and injury or disaster at the most. Contrary to the philosophy of those who say, "I can do what I want as long as I don't harm anyone," we need basic rules and regulations that provide structure for our societal well-being.

But not everyone responds to laws the same way. Some people gladly go on with life, and for the most part, enjoy obeying them. Others cringe under the law, meticulously trying to obey every detail, fearful of what might happen if they don't. Still others operate above the law, arrogantly disregarding it when it's to their advantage, even when neighbors suffer as a consequence.

I get a kick out of the imagination and plight of Dave Bresnahan, a backup catcher for the Double-A Williamsport (Pennsylvania) Bills. On August 31, 1987, his team was hosting the Reading Phillies. No one else knew he had concealed a potato in his pocket.

> Bresnahan was catching the first game of a double-header when, with two out and a runner on third in the fifth inning, he hurled what looked like a baseball past the third baseman and into left field. The runner, Rick Lundblade, trotted home only to be tagged out at the plate.
>
> [No one] was amused when the deception was revealed. [The umpire] ruled the run had scored on a catcher's error, despite Bresnahan's protests. "I'm saying, 'I tagged him out. There's no rule, I looked it up.'"[3]

But there was a rule, unwritten though it was, even with baseball's thick rule book. The escapade ended Bresnahan's baseball career and made him an instant celebrity. His number was retired due to his celebrity.

How do Christians treat rules and regulations? We categorize some as church law and others as civil law. Some we follow in public but not in private. Some appear more important than others, and some are clearly out of date. And where there aren't any, we create our own to fill in gaps.

Does the Christian live above the law or under it? Or is there another way? Certainly the church is more than a religious affiliation in which something is "allowed," more than a social club whose welcome to membership is a detailed list of requirements. But the church is notorious for its laws and decrees, its traditions and doctrines. We divide into camps that champion conservative or liberal views. We position ourselves in denominations and movements that claim superiority over others. And we construct codes of law that rival our civil systems. Meanwhile, we aim a confusing message at those who seek God's righteousness for themselves and their communities. Pastor Firman Gingerich speaks of this in his own spiritual pilgrimage.

> I grew up in a large family, rural community, southeastern Iowa, the youngest of a family of eight. I learned at a very young age that if I did well in school I'd be rewarded; if I did my chores at home, I'd be rewarded; if I did both, I'd get to go along with my dad on Saturday to town, to get the groceries. Then we'd go into this little Bible and banana and candy store and I'd get a stick of licorice, and I'd get to stop by the library and take a book. As a ten, twelve-year-old, that's about all I needed in life. Life was good.
>
> These lessons about doing well and then being rewarded for it were easy then for me to bridge to my faith. I heard a lot of sermons as a child about being right with God. So as hard as I was working to please

my family and do well in my family, that's about as
hard as I was working to please God and do well
there. But I also lived with a long list of shoulds and
have-to's. You know those horrible S's of sin—sex,
swearing, and smoking—stay away from those. And I
did. And they aren't bad to stay away from. The problem was, I developed a faith view based on trying to
please God. If I did all these kinds of things, then God
would bless me, because I was faithful.

And so as a teenager, I started noticing that there
was a disconnect between what I had in my heart and
what people saw out there. And I've since learned that
there is a term for that—it's called cognitive dissonance. Cognitive dissonance is a theory that talks
about the gap between what we believe and what we
do, a gap between our faith and our actions, a gap
between Sunday morning and Monday morning.

But this troubled me a lot as a late teen and into
my early twenties. I pretended so hard, I tried so hard,
to be perfect in school. I pretended never to be angry.
In fact, I only got into one fight all the way through
seminary, but that doesn't say that internally I wasn't
hostile or angry. In some ways the public self and the
personal self was very conflicted. And I remember
being very troubled in the late sixties during the
Vietnam War era, being very angry at the church
because they wouldn't be more proactive in giving a
peace witness. All they wanted to do was talk about
my long hair.

But inside, even in the midst of all that, I yearned
for a different kind of relationship to God—a relationship to God that wasn't based on works, a relationship to God that would get me off of this treadmill
of ever trying harder and knowing I couldn't succeed.

I think if I look back on my life in my twenties
[and] thirties, I sort of moved from time to time from
two extremes. The one was from complete apathy—I
can't make it anyway, so why try? To hell with the

church. And I had those years—the harder you try, the bigger the disconnect. Then other days I would say, I'm going to get this right. I'm going to love God with all my heart. I'm going to love everybody. Just watch me! And I would try harder and harder and harder.[4]

In the Sermon on the Mount, Jesus tells the crowds that they will never enter the kingdom of the heavens unless their righteousness goes beyond that of the scribes and Pharisees (see Matthew 5:20). For many years, the seeming inconsistency of those vivid words bothered me. Here was Jesus, the radical teacher, proclaiming that he had come not to abolish the law but to fulfill it (see 5:13). Then he finishes off his remarks by saying that unless our righteousness surpasses that of the scribes and Pharisees, we'll never enter the kingdom of the heavens. How could Jesus make such a pronouncement, when at the same time he was constantly in conflict with those same religious leaders because they kept the law so vengefully? Jesus now appears to be singing a different tune. It sounds as if we must beat the scribes and Pharisees at their own game. But who could dream of fulfilling the law better than those who are experts in the law? Along with Pastor Gingerich, we wonder if there's something we are missing.

The key to understanding Jesus' statement also unlocks the whole Sermon on the Mount: God's righteousness as Jesus reveals it. Jesus came to earth and took on human flesh to show us what God is like, not to deify the human situation. The scribes and Pharisees understood righteousness from their traditional perspective, which was based mainly on rules and regulations. Jesus went beyond their understanding to the intentions of God's law and showed how application of God's righteousness transcends the limited scope of the scribes and Pharisees. The direct and essential teaching of Jesus in the Sermon on the Mount portrays what it means to live not under the law or above it, but *beyond* the law.

So if lists of do's and don'ts promote a misconception of

the Christian faith, how do we move beyond that? What does *righteousness* mean, anyway? As significant as it is, righteousness is a concept that always seems to need explanation. Basically its meaning is contained in its first syllable, *right.* Its use in the Hebrew scriptures carries the meaning of "just," as in "justice." In God's kingdom there is rightness when everything is in place, when everything is happening as it should, when everything is shaped by the will of God. That is what we call righteousness.

Let me come at it another way by putting it in personal and physical terms. By my junior year of college, I had already been playing piano for years and had reached what I thought was a high level of technical proficiency. Then I was introduced to a technique of piano playing that would significantly affect the rest of my life. This new approach to playing the piano showed me that it was not the fingers alone that played the piano but that other muscles and members of the body were intricately involved. My teacher, Henry J. Black, showed me how the fingers were an extension of the arm, the arm an extension of the shoulder, and the shoulder an extension of the rest of the body. To expect just the fingers to operate the keys was to invite a tightening of the muscles, producing a metallic and mechanical sound, rather than bringing forth the wide range of expressive tones available from the piano.

I can still remember Mr. Black's grin and chuckle as he instructed me to do "arm drops," an exercise to learn this technique. I would hold my arm in the air with my hand hanging down over the keyboard, then let my arm free fall until the chosen finger would make contact with a key. At that point, the arch that was created from the end of the finger through the raised hand and on to the wrist then the forearm to the elbow allowed the weight of the arm to play the key. In simplest terms, that is how the fingers can function as an extension of the arm, and the amount of arm weight in motion can help determine the tonal variety and volume of sound. The fingers and their muscles alone do not strike the keys, but they serve to distribute the energy that is generated by the falling weight of the arm, and beyond that, by the flowing motion of the rest of the body.

Some interesting things happened to me through this revelation. Mr. Black cautioned that as I began to adopt this way of playing, I might initially feel a loss of control at the keyboard. It could feel as if my playing were becoming sloppy. Without the former tightness in my hands and fingers, my brain would tell me I was not in control. But Mr. Black said I shouldn't worry, because this phase would continue only until I learned how to respond to what was going on.

And that is precisely what happened. I struggled with the sloppy stage and wondered how I would ever gain control. But as the new approach began to affect my technique, my thinking and actions began to reprogram themselves, and I began to develop a new idea of what it means to play the piano. My playing was becoming clear and free, with a relaxed control that was not suppressing facility but encouraging it.

But it wasn't just my piano technique that was changing. My whole musicianship was undergoing a transformation. As I more and more applied the new technique, my ears began opening to new sounds. Instead of being satisfied with only a generic piano sound, I began to hear an immeasurable variation of tonal qualities, a concept formerly foreign to me. During that year I went to a piano concert by the young, prize-winning Belgian musician Michel Block and was completely mesmerized by his sensitive, magnificent performance. A door had begun to open for me. I started to hear music in a way I had not, and I realized that my musical discernment was growing.

An amusing thing happened the following spring as I played softball on our class team. I was hitting the ball with more power than ever before. It surprised me and pleased my teammates. As I pondered this, I attributed my new success in hitting the ball to the way I was learning to use my whole body to play the piano. As I swung at the ball, I was letting my arms become an extension of my relaxed shoulders, which were in turn an extension of my whole body. When that coordinated energy found its way to the point of bat meeting ball, the ball traveled a long way.

What was happening? In both piano playing and softball hitting, I was allowing my body to function as it should, all parts working as one, not emphasizing one part over the other. In softball, the idea was to play ball, not to control every movement. It was only later that I was to learn of Timothy Gallway's concept of "the inner game" and how the body needs the freedom to perform as it naturally wants to (self 2), instead of being controlled by one's thinking and planning (self 1). In piano, the dramatic change in my approach to technique, and therefore to the larger scope of music, was a harbinger of what I was to discover in other areas of life, notably in the righteousness of God's kingdom.

For piano playing, fingers are necessary, but they alone cannot play the piano. True musicians see fingers for what they are: important links in the whole process of making music. Fingers do not stand alone. If facility or control by the fingers becomes the goal that performers and listeners crave, the music itself suffers. If people are interested mainly in how fast or flamboyantly or "correctly" the music is performed, technique itself becomes the reason for the performance. But when the performer's technique finds its rightful place, it becomes an essential, and sometimes invisible, channel through which the music itself can flow.

Righteousness comes like that. Righteousness flows from its source in God and expresses itself through the body of Christ on earth. Righteousness is the divine "music" that inspires and motivates and gives life to all that takes place in God's will. Just as the fingers do not by themselves make music, our various expressions of God's righteousness are not themselves righteous. They are avenues through which God's "music" comes. Fingers cannot dictate what the music is, although they sometimes try—just as our self-righteous deeds cannot dictate what righteousness is, although we sometimes think they can.

Whatever we do as Christians is possible only because of God's righteousness, not because of what we do or who we are. Our identity and purpose come from relating to the source. If I want to write a Christian song, it doesn't happen just by throwing in the name of Jesus here and there. If I want to be a Christian singer, it doesn't happen just by imitating the sounds and movements of well-known Christian singers. Or, if I want to be a Christian, period, it doesn't happen by trying to be good or honest or by going to church—by following rules. It is only when I connect with the one who makes me Christian, allowing his life to flow through me, that my songs and my whole life express Christlikeness, no matter who I am or where I live or what kind of "music" I perform. That's righteousness.

Often we want to control things from our end and make righteousness happen, instead of letting the source of righteousness inform us and guide us and flow through us. When people go away from home to attend a special church assembly or conference, they often participate in inspiring times of worship. Sometimes they ask for copies of the music, readings, or plays that were used, so they can reproduce that worship in their home congregation. But what happens at the assembly simply cannot be transferred back home. The worship is not something to be "bottled" and taken along. The energy, the passion, the experience, cannot be reproduced. The people and places are different, expectations are different, and energies generated in each group are different. It could well be that some of the songs and litanies used at the meeting would work in home congregations, but if they are taken home as "righteous" things to make exciting worship happen, only the "fingers" will be visible, and the real "music" will not be heard. True—that is, relevant—worship flows from the one who inspires the planners, leaders, and worshippers wherever they gather, whether at the assembly or at home. It is only when we get in touch with the source of worship that real worship can happen.

New pots and pans won't make me a good cook (believe me!). The right kind of cleats and slacks and clubs won't make someone a good golfer either, although good equipment might help. And cool-looking guitars and drums won't create a rocking band, although we could have a lot of fun jamming. So it is with righteousness. Whenever we try to create and control God's righteousness by what we do and say, we put our own ideas and standards above God's. But whenever we allow ourselves as the body of Christ to function freely, to let all parts of the body join in response to the action of God, the whole body becomes the course through which God's righteousness can lavishly flow.

The legendary orchestra conductor Arturo Toscanini once told a trumpet player, "God tells me how the music should sound, but you stand in the way." In the kingdom of the heavens, God's righteousness is the music—the source and reason for the concert. The body of Christ is the performer. If any parts of the body arrogantly "stand in the way," then those "fingers" self-righteously draw attention to themselves and their power, and proclaim a restricted and warped view of the kingdom of the heavens. After the apostle Peter visited and lodged with Cornelius, an uncircumcised Gentile, he was cornered by Jerusalem believers who were certain he had broken the law of God's covenant. But Peter responded that God had baptized Cornelius and his friends with the same Spirit the believers had received at Pentecost, and then added, "Who was I to think that I could stand in God's way?" (Acts 11:17 TNIV).

Body parts that shape righteousness according to their own limited understanding do not embrace the wider, deeper essence that is God's righteousness. However, on the other side of the coin, no individual, congregation, denomination, or church should be a Toscanini and claim to have a corner on God. It is an absolute necessity for the entire body of Christ to hear, nurture, and reveal the immeasurable riches of righteousness that flow through us from their origin in God.

I was sitting next to a table in the hallway of Erie County Prison, behind the first set of locked doors. I was waiting to be taken to what was called an attorney-client room for a pastoral visit with an inmate. I had my Bible on the table next to me. Soon another man joined me and sat down on the other side of the table to wait his turn. He laid his briefcase on the table. After a short time I asked, "Are you an attorney?"

"Yes," he answered, "and I assume you are not one since you have a Bible." We grinned at each other.

The scribes were the lawyers of their day, experts expected to see that the law was lived out properly. Lawyers are specialists who study, teach, and work with the law. They do not make law, but it is their duty to be versed in the law and to put it into practice, seeing that what has been written into law is appropriately applied. When Jesus had finished his Sermon, Matthew reports that the crowds were astounded at his teaching "because he taught as one who had authority, and not as their teachers of the law" (7:29 TNIV). The people with whom Jesus ate and drank lived by the Law of Moses, which served as their religious and civil code. As the crowds heard Jesus teaching the law of God's righteousness, they were fully aware that he was not teaching law on the same level as their lawyers, but as one who had authority to actually reinterpret the law.

In the language of our own day, it is judges who have authority to set precedent by creating a decision that changes a former ruling of law and establishes a new rule. In those terms, the concluding verses of chapter 7 might read, "Now when Jesus finished these words, the crowds were amazed at his teaching, for he was teaching them as a judge establishing precedent, and not as their lawyers" (verses 28-29 PKC).

The scribes didn't have a clue. They were unable to give people real righteousness. They were teaching the law as rules to create righteousness, instead of helping people find God's goodness. They were absorbed with the technique of obtaining righteousness and could not see beyond the law to its living source. Their tightness got in the way. And the Pharisees, the religious elite, were preoccupied with preserving their status by making sure no one else was able to obey the whole law perfectly, as they professed to do. When Jesus said that one could enter the kingdom of the heavens only by surpassing the righteousness of the scribes and Pharisees (5:20), it looked hopeless for regular people. Who could do that? Who could be more righteous than the scribes and Pharisees? But it raised questions for the scribes and Pharisees too. Was Jesus saying their righteousness was not enough? Could there be a righteousness beyond theirs?

The scribes and Pharisees showed that it can be difficult for anyone to give up crippling and self-centered control. But change is possible, as I learned when I gave up my old piano technique for the new. Although for a while I felt as though I had no control through my fingers, gradually that feeling was transformed into a new way of understanding, communicating, and enjoying the music that stands beyond any kind of technique. Instead of letting my tight fingers choke off the rest of my body, causing me to miss the real music entirely, I was now listening to the music and learning to let it flow through my whole body.

Throughout the Sermon on the Mount, Jesus calls for a life of righteousness that befits and establishes his Father's kingdom. At the center of the discourse he instructs his followers to pray to the Father in the heavens: "Your kingdom come, your will be done, on earth as it is in heaven" (6:10). At another place Jesus urges his hearers to make God's kingdom—God's righteousness—their top priority and not to let everyday concerns get in the way (see 6:33). In his closing remarks he reminds everyone that there is nothing they can do on their own that will get them into the kingdom of the heavens; entry is possible only by doing the will of their Father in the heavens (see 7:21-23). The Father's will is not accomplished by fulfilling laws, but by doing righteousness; not by "doing well and then being rewarded for it," as Firman Gingerich remembered, but by living beyond the law.

God's righteousness is not stored away to be unwrapped at some future celebration. Jesus himself announced the immediate presence of God's kingdom and its righteousness as he echoed the words of John the Baptist: "Everybody change! The kingdom of the heavens is here!" (3:2; 4:17 PKC). Then he sent his disciples out to proclaim the same good news: "The kingdom of the heavens is here!" (10:7 PKC).

If God's righteousness is available now, what does it mean for us to live from within that righteousness that is beyond the law? In terms of the Sermon on the Mount, when everything is in place, when everything is happening as it should, and when everything is shaped by the will of God, God's righteousness is seen and heard in all its splendor, and everyone gives glory to the Father in the heavens (see 5:16; 6:1). When we seek first the righteousness of God's kingdom, everything else joyously falls into place (see 6:33). And there is wonderful music.

For Discussion

Do you maintain rules for yourself that you hold as sacred and untouchable—that is, to which there are no exceptions? Identify rules that you interpret somewhat freely in your own favor but apply more strictly with regard to others (for instance, relating to school, work, driving, church, income tax).

Can Abraham's act of planning to kill Isaac be considered as righteousness? Can such a negative intent be considered positive? See Genesis 15:6 and 22:1-19; Galatians 2:15-16; James 2:20-26.

Define righteousness. Is it tangible? Can it be seen? Is it an action?

— 2 —

Kingdom and Community
Did You Say 'Heavens'?

One evening in Bible study, Jim remarked, "If the law against murder were dropped, we wouldn't all run out and kill someone." That got our attention. Jim was right, of course. None of us there would do such a thing, and neither would most people. We were looking at the Sermon on the Mount where Jesus says, "You have heard that it was said to those of ancient times, 'You shall not murder'; and 'whoever murders shall be liable to judgment.' But I say to you that if you are angry with a brother or sister, you will be liable to judgment" (5:21-22).

No, we wouldn't all run out and kill someone. But get angry? That's another story. What does Jesus have in mind? In chapter 4 we'll look more closely at his unsettling statement. But first we need to ask what *law* means and how it relates to living God's righteousness in everyday life.

I asked the Bible class, "Would it be Christian for me to drive at seventy-five in a fifty-five-mile-per-hour zone?" The question hit home for Laura Lee and she responded with her patented little gasp and knowing chuckle, seeing that the Christian life could relate to everyday driving. So if speed limits were dropped, would we all run out and speed?

You could make the argument that if there were no speed limits, you would not be speeding. The same could be said about murder. If there were no law against it, how could it be murder? Or is everyone so conditioned by the Ten Commandments that

35

we know it is wrong to murder? The question is this: Is it law that makes something right or wrong, or is there something beyond the law from which the law itself derives?

A pastor friend told me of a young man who is especially outspoken about his Christian faith, but he doesn't put evangelistic bumper stickers on his car so people won't get the wrong impression from his driving. I commend the young man for his honesty and for seeing a connection between righteousness and everyday life. Somehow he knows that his actions are not compatible with what he says.

My guess is that many Christians regularly drive above the speed limit. Traffic laws are the kind of rules we assume we can break as long as we don't get caught. Driving over the speed limit is not driving beyond the law, but driving above the law. Speed limits are laws established for safety. If we obey the speed limit just because it is the law, we might be tempted to say, "Lord, look at the good things we are doing!" (see 7:22). But kingdom people have the choice to live beyond the law in God's goodness. Speed laws are not posted to irk us or to keep us from pushing our cars to the extraordinary speeds they can go. They do not exist to make our commute to work take longer or to add travel time to holiday trips. They are for safety.

Safety is the "righteousness" within which speed limits are created. What if I said, "Today I am going to drive safely"? What if I left for work five or ten minutes earlier? What if I drove so I could avoid hitting a child darting into the street? What if I drove in a way that respected other drivers? Then speed limits would actually serve as an aid to my driving, not as impediments. Instead of grudgingly following rules, I would be driving for the reasons speed limits were created in the first place. By driving to fulfill the "righteousness" of safety, I would be driving beyond the law.

A truly good citizen would want to drive within the speed limits for the reasons they were created. What if all professing Christians drove that way? Would traffic fatalities dramatically drop? Would driving become less stressful? Would road rage decrease? Would the Christian witness become stronger?

Jesus had the kingdom on his mind. Early in his ministry he was tempted by the devil to turn the gift of God's generous righteousness into an oppressive system of arrogant and selfish control. In the wilderness the devil had taken the newly baptized Son of God to a high mountain to show him "all the kingdoms of the world and their glory" (Matthew 4:8 NKJV), telling Jesus that he could have the whole world eating out of his hand if only he would pledge his allegiance to the devil. But Jesus did not want to command all the kingdoms of the world. He rebuked Satan by quoting Deuteronomy 6:13, which says that only God is to be worshipped and served. Jesus' mission was to choose and demonstrate the servant posture of God's righteousness and to bring that goodness alive through those who would join his kingdom. Even in the face of death by crucifixion, Jesus resolutely confirmed his mission when he told Pilate, the Roman governor, "My kingdom is not of this world" (John 18:36 NKJV). The magnificent music and thrilling cheers of Handel's "Hallelujah" chorus echo the strain:

> The kingdom of this world is become
> the Kingdom of our Lord and of his Christ,
> and he will reign for ever and ever. . . .
> King of Kings and Lord of Lords.
> (Revelation 11:15; 19:16 NET)

That is Christ's mission, that is Christ's purpose—not to "capture" the world, but to invite the kingdom of this world into an existence transformed by God's righteousness.

Within the "kingdom of this world" are innumerable other kingdoms or systems. Obvious ones are nations; ethnicities; political systems such as communism, monarchy, or democracy; and religions such as Christianity, Judaism,

Islam, and Hinduism. Kingdoms of the world are not evil merely because they are of the world. Every kingdom has its own traditions or laws that characterize its particular system of organization. If the kingdom is an ethnic group, for instance, its members adhere to the specific cultural expectations and habits of that system. If a kingdom is an established nation, it has a specified political government, and the intention of its faithful citizens is to obey the law of the land, whatever that may be.

The intention of faithful citizens in the United States is to follow and obey its laws. Because the U.S. Constitution is the basis of law and government structure in the United States, it could for our purposes be called the "righteousness" of the United States. In American democracy, the actions of individuals and governments are ultimately judged in some way by how they measure up to the Constitution. If people come into conflict over matters of authority or points of law, the courts determine what the Constitution means. When someone commits a crime, especially one that shocks the public, we hear the cry for justice, and law enforcement pledges that justice will be done. Justice occurs when the law is fulfilled and criminals are punished for doing wrong, while those who are innocent of crime are left alone.

From time to time, depending on what is under consideration, a law may not line up with the moral beliefs of certain individuals or groups. But the laws decide for the country what is right and wrong, good and bad. Such determinations, we should remind ourselves, are legal but may not necessarily be moral according to some points of view. It is also true that people can be outrageously nasty and disagreeable but still obey the law; they are seen as good though we may not like them. In contrast, pleasant neighbors who keep their yard beautifully manicured may secretly be cheating on their taxes; we may like them, but they might be criminals. The law is no respecter of persons.

The rule of law may not always result in what everyone thinks is right. Take, for example, the heart-wrenching case of Theresa Schiavo, whose lingering demise was a divisive issue that dominated the press for a time in 2005. Schiavo had suffered severe damage in February 1990 when her heart stopped beating for several minutes and oxygen to her brain was cut off. Until her eventual death on March 31, 2005, life for her continued in what doctors called a persistent vegetative state. She received nourishment through a feeding tube. Because her husband and parents disagreed on whether she would have desired to be kept alive artificially, the case went to court. Those proceedings evolved into a political quarrel in which even the president of the United States became involved. People were torn over the many questions the case raised. Should her feeding tube be removed? When does life end? Where are the voices of reason and love? What does God want?

Finally the feeding tube was removed permanently. The law had the last word, even though people in authority at times ruled in ways with which they may have personally disagreed. That extraordinary case revealed exasperating difficulties involving moral, emotional, and legal complexities of law. However, as we noted, the U.S. Constitution ultimately guides the laws by which the citizens of the United States abide. Its "righteousness" must be fulfilled. And it was the absolute supremacy of the Constitution that shaped the procedures and ultimate outcome of the Schiavo case. The unanimous ruling handed down by the Supreme Court of Florida, September 23, 2004, stated:

> We are a nation of laws and we must govern our decisions by the rule of law and not by our own emotions. Our hearts can fully comprehend the grief so fully demonstrated by Theresa's family members on this record. But our hearts are not the law. What is in the Constitution always must prevail over emotion.[1]

As tough and as controversial as the Schiavo lawsuit proved to be, we do know that the final ruling was determined on a legal basis and was therefore just—or good—according to the "righteousness" of the Constitution. Not that everyone agrees with the outcome. It is unfortunate that when our courts hand down decisions, somebody wins and somebody loses. Whatever is written in the books must be carried out, no matter what that means for any of us involved. Like it or not, that is justice.

But citizens of the United States harbor contradictory views on such "righteousness." After the June 26, 2002, court ruling that the phrase "under God" in the pledge of allegiance makes it unconstitutional, strident voices arose as our country reacted. One man seems to have spoken for many people: "The people that say this stuff, that don't like this country, they can get the hell out of here. . . . The three G's made this country: God, guns and guts. If you have a problem with that, I'm a problem solver."[2]

Although church groups use different language, they have been just as opinionated, whether for the ruling or against it. One editor of a church periodical lamented that our culture too often sets the agenda for Christians, as seen in the several months leading up to the 2004 presidential election in America. In the church, he noted, we fight each other using categories taken from the wider society, such as calling each other "conservative Republicans" or "liberal Democrats." He asks, "What ever happened to 'brothers and sisters in Christ'?"[3]

Arnold C. Roth, a friend and former pastoral colleague of mine, tells a story his father told him.

> There was an election at the church. As the family went home with the horse and buggy (that gave them more time), the children were discussing for whom they had voted for the various positions. Each time they had established their own votes, they called to

their father, "Who did you want, Dad?" and added that to their tallies. After several discussions, they noticed their father always chose the person who was elected. "Dad, how did you know who would be elected? You always voted for that one." Their father replied, "You didn't ask me who I voted for. You asked me who I wanted. I want the person the church chose, even though I didn't always vote for them."

As good or helpful or beautiful as a kingdom might be, no kingdom of this world compares to the kingdom Jesus brought among us. The kingdom of Christ and of God is beyond the scope of earthly kingdoms because it is not limited by human understandings of time and space or by any earthly kingdom's "righteousness." The heavenly kingdom brings the righteousness of God onto the human scene so that God's goodness might flow through the earthly body of Christ. And that can happen only as people become followers of Christ. Earthly kingdoms may provide a satisfactory existence for you and me from time to time, but none of them is based on living God's righteousness. I agree with Philip Yancey, who wrote,

> A state government can shut down stores and theaters on Sunday, but it cannot compel worship. It can arrest and punish KKK murderers but cannot cure their hatred, much less teach them love. It can pass laws making divorce more difficult but cannot force husbands to love their wives and wives their husbands. It can give subsidies to the poor but cannot force the rich to show them compassion and justice. It can ban adultery but not lust, theft but not covetousness, cheating but not pride. It can encourage virtue but not holiness.[4]

Jesus came offering a peaceable kingdom that welcomes "citizens" from all earthly kingdoms. "The kingdom of the heavens is here!" (Matthew 4:17 PKC), Jesus proclaimed, and in his life he revealed the abundant riches of God's righteousness that characterize that very kingdom. Of the whole

New Testament, the Gospel of Matthew is the only place where the plural *heavens* is found in a phrase linked with *kingdom*. Recent English translations of Matthew, however, use only the singular *heaven*, even where the Greek text has "kingdom of the heavens" or "Father in the heavens."

On the surface it may seem unimportant, even picky, to cite the difference, but I am curious to know why Matthew would use *heaven* as well as *heavens*. I cannot think it was merely sloppy writing; Matthew must have visualized a difference. In Matthew 5:18, for example, Jesus speaks of heaven (singular) and earth, which will pass away, and in the familiar words of the Lord's Prayer he uses the singular: "Your will be done, on earth as it is in heaven" (6:10). The singular *heaven* forms a contrast with earth so that heaven sounds far off somewhere, away from us, a place where we desire to live eternally, the place where God is, where we hope to walk the streets of gold. But when Jesus announces that the kingdom of the heavens is here now, it doesn't sound far away. It sounds accessible. Dallas Willard points out that God watches and acts precisely from the space immediately around us.

> Nothing—no human being or institution, no time, no space, no spiritual being, no event—stands between God and those who trust him. The "heavens" are always there with you no matter what, and the "first heaven," in biblical terms, is precisely the atmosphere or air that surrounds your body.[5]

"The kingdom of the heavens" suggests an interrelationship between earth and heaven, rather than a contrast. It represents God's kingdom in its reachable form—the air around us, a context we know, a present reality—and is close, tangible, and identifiable. Matthew's use of both the singular and the plural encourages me to expand my thinking about God's boundless space and immediate presence. "The kingdom of the heavens" allows me to freely accept God's kingdom as both within reach and distant, an earth and heaven that intersect in the present. Indeed, as the apostle Paul says in Philippians 3:20 (in the Greek), "Our citizenship is in the heavens" (PKC).[6]

We may find it difficult to accept that God can actually be present among us or that we can welcome God as a genuine part of our workaday world. But we cannot let our image of a distant God in a faraway heaven negatively color our perceptions. The Father in the heavens does make himself available to us and does desire our presence. As I have personally applied the plural *heavens* where it appears in Matthew, our Father in the heavens has emerged for me as a near-at-hand, encompassing presence. I intellectually know and regularly confess that God lives with us by means of the Holy Spirit, who dwells in the living temple built among us in Jesus Christ. Why not live that way?

Alongside such a wondrous truth, it is saddening that, for some Christians, referring to God as Father has become troublesome, though the reasons for it are understandable. Many men and women have been treated poorly, abandoned, or abused by their fathers. It is regrettable that in such sensitive situations some persons are virtually forced by church people to use *Father* as a title for God. Similarly, it is not helpful, Christian, or even correct to use the concept of God as Father in a disparaging way with reference to females or in an affirmative way with reference to males. Given the somewhat injured meaning of *Father* among Christians, I ask that we explore the concept of our Father in the heavens from the perspective of biblical use, rather than from our own emotions. The Bible is clear that God rises far above any human categorization of sex or other images. *Father* is a term of relationship with God that comes through faith in Jesus Christ. To call God "Father" does not make God a male, and it is small of us to grant men unilateral hierarchical authority based on this mistaken notion of male privilege. The following observation by Thomas R. Yoder Neufeld provides a helpful reminder from Ephesians 4:32—5:1 of how all God's children might best live together, no matter who they are:

> *All* the saints, men and women alike, including fathers, are to be tenderhearted, forgiving, kind, and loving to the utmost. A notion of fatherhood premised on such a foundation would ill fit a patriarchy slanted to serve the interests of fathers at the expense of mothers and children.[7]

In Matthew the kingdom of the heavens implies the Hebrew realization of *shalom* (peace, well-being) and the early church's practice of *koinonia* (fellowship, community)—the "peaceable kingdom" Isaiah envisioned (see Isaiah 11:1-11). Just as God formerly had established his righteousness in the kingdom of Israel, now God through Christ was inaugurating a kingdom free from the boundaries of earthly kingdoms. This new kingdom would be a community of God's righteousness based not on the law as given through Moses, but on the grace and truth of God as disclosed in Jesus (see John 1:14-18). The prophet Jeremiah envisioned such a relationship.

> "But this is the new covenant I will make with the people of Israel on that day," says the LORD. "*I will put my instructions deep within them, and I will write them on their hearts.* I will be their God, and they will be my people. And they will not need to teach their neighbors, nor will they need to teach their relatives, saying, 'You should know the LORD.' For everyone, from the least to the greatest, will already know me," says the LORD. "And I will forgive their wickedness, and I will never again remember their sins." (Jeremiah 31:33-34 NLT, italics added)

Centuries later, the apostle Paul announced that God's righteousness had been accomplished in Christ Jesus. We no longer labor under the Mosaic Law, he says, but have become the righteousness of God (see 2 Corinthians 5:21; Ephesians 4:24). With impassioned words he tells the Galatians,

> Before the way of faith in Christ was available to us,
> we were placed under guard by the law. We were kept
> in protective custody, so to speak, until the way of
> faith was revealed.
>
> Let me put it another way. The law was our
> guardian until Christ came; it protected us until we
> could be made right with God through faith. And now
> that the way of faith has come, we no longer need the
> law as our guardian. For you are all children of God
> through faith in Christ Jesus. (Galatians 3:23-26 NLT)

God created humankind to live as residents in a garden
of Eden, but you and I and our fellow human beings have
messed up that design, and we keep messing it up. God's plan
to cover our sin is salvation through Jesus Christ. God rescues us from that mess. The prophetic vision of God's *shalom*
in Isaiah's "peaceable kingdom" may appear to be only a
utopian dream, as far off as what we consider heaven to be.
But I do not believe for one moment that such a kingdom
refers only to the heaven we hope to enter at the consummation of the world on judgment day.

In Jesus' timeless story in Matthew 25:31-46, when the
Son of Man divides the people as a shepherd separates the
sheep from the goats, he says to those who have served him
in righteousness, "Come, you who are blessed by my Father,
inherit the kingdom prepared for you from the foundation of
the world" (verse 34 NET). From before the beginning of the
world, God planned for divine love and graciousness, peace
and righteousness, to be the everyday way of life, not the
exception. The sinful world is the exception, a rebellious
choice made in arrogance by human beings. Heaven is not an
afterthought, nor is the kingdom of the heavens, which
promises life in a garden of Eden lost earlier because of sin.

That heavenly community began to take shape visually in
the wake of Peter's mighty sermon on Pentecost. The listeners were "cut to the heart," and when they asked how to set

right their response to Jesus, whom they had crucified, Peter told them to repent and be baptized. Then he warned them that to follow Christ they needed to remove themselves from their present kingdoms. He urged them to save themselves from their crooked generation: "Get out while you can; get out of this sick and stupid culture!" (Acts 2:40 Msg).

Three thousand people did leave their kingdoms that day and were baptized into the kingdom of the heavens where "they devoted themselves to the apostles' teaching and to fellowship, to the breaking of bread and to prayer" (2:42 TNIV). Here the English word *fellowship* translates the Greek word *koinonia*, a New Testament word that came to signify the peace, fellowship, and mission of the kingdom of the heavens. The meaning of *koinonia* is so rich it cannot be captured by only the one word *fellowship*, but also means communion, sharing, partnership, and participation. More than that, koinonia is a gift of God that comes to life because Christ is present. Koinonia is the incarnation of God in the midst of the congregation. Koinonia is "Emmanuel," God with us. Koinonia is Christ in community.

In the Sermon on the Mount, Jesus taught that those who commit themselves to doing the will of the Father in the heavens are the ones who unselfishly seek first the kingdom of the heavens and its righteousness, and let earthly necessities fall into place after that (see 6:33). The kingdoms of the world, as good as they might be, are not agents of God to bring righteousness and salvation to a lost world. That mission is given to the kingdom of the heavens, whose members are "ambassadors for Christ" (2 Corinthians 5:20) and which is accomplished through salvation and redemption in Jesus the Christ, who is the head of the church: "The church, you see, is not peripheral to the world; the world is peripheral to the church. The church is Christ's body, in which he speaks and acts, by which he fills everything with his presence" (Ephesians 1:23 Msg).

It was my privilege to become involved in the Christian movement called Koinonia, which is ecumenical in membership and led by laypeople. It is similar to groups such as Chrysalis, Kairos, Walk to Emmaus, Footsteps, Great Banquet, and the Episcopal Cursillo, all of which are descended in some way from the Roman Catholic experience called Cursillo ("short course" in Spanish). In briefest terms, each group offers intensive spiritual retreats over extended weekends. After participating in a Koinonia weekend as candidates, participants become members and may then serve in various capacities of planning and leadership.

Since Koinonia retreats are lay led, one way pastors may assist is by serving as spiritual directors, a position I filled a number of times with Koinonia of Erie County, Pennsylvania, and Koinonia of Jamestown and Chautauqua County, New York. Always I saw candidates led to confession, renewal, or commitment by the koinonia experienced there, and I was moved by their testimonies: "I see the Lord in everyone's face"; "The love here is phenomenal"; "I thought I knew all about love—I didn't have a clue"; "I won't be the same person ever again." My dream for Koinonia is for it to work itself out of a job. Wouldn't it be great if the ministry of Koinonia and other renewal movements became so effective that no more retreats were needed? As a result, every congregation of God's people would become an exuberant body of God's love and fellowship and generosity.

Christ in community. That's what the church is about! The kingdom of the heavens promises the creation of a new garden of Eden here and now. In creating Eve to be with Adam, God created community. The new creation in Christ is a fellowship of redeemed people, children of God with new hearts, a community in which "everything old has passed away; see, everything has become new!" (2 Corinthians 5:17).

The Supreme Court of Florida wrote that "our hearts are not the law." True. But in the kingdom of the heavens, God's heart *is* the law. God's righteousness is the "constitution" of the kingdom of the heavens. From within God's abundant goodness flow lavish grace and love along with peace and fellowship, all of which shape the community of Christ. We obey traffic laws because they help us do what we genuinely want to do. If everyone drove that way, we wouldn't need traffic laws, just reminders. When the community of Christ lives according to the righteousness of God, then the laws of God's righteousness are fulfilled. If all Christian communities lived the mind of Christ, we genuinely would live beyond the law.

For Discussion

Identify and describe "kingdoms" that exist in your world—their boundaries, nature, expectations. How do you relate to them? Are they good, bad, neutral?

Come on now! You mean to say that driving the speed limit really relates to being a Christian? And that a good citizen would not disobey the speed limit? Well, what do you think?

The English word *saints* comes from the Greek word for "holy ones." What does *holy* mean? Why do you think New Testament Christians are referred to as saints? And why does the New Testament always use *saints* in the plural, never the singular?

— 3 —

Beatitudes and Blessings
The Future Is Now

Blessed are the poor in spirit, for theirs is the kingdom of [the heavens].

Blessed are those who mourn, for they will be comforted.

Blessed are the meek, for they will inherit the earth.

Blessed are those who hunger and thirst for righteousness, for they will be filled.

Blessed are the merciful, for they will receive mercy.

Blessed are the pure in heart, for they will see God.

Blessed are the peacemakers, for they will be called children of God.

Blessed are those who are persecuted for righteousness' sake, for theirs is the kingdom of [the heavens].

Blessed are you when people revile you and persecute you and utter all kinds of evil against you falsely on my account. Rejoice and be glad, for your reward is great in [the heavens], for in the same way they persecuted the prophets who were before you.

You are the salt of the earth; but if salt has lost its taste, how can its saltiness be restored? It is no longer good for anything, but is thrown out and trampled under foot.

You are the light of the world. A city built on a hill cannot be hid. No one after lighting a lamp puts it under the bushel basket, but on the lampstand, and it gives light to all in the house. In the same way, let your light shine before others, so that they máy see your good works and give glory to your Father in [the heavens]. (Matthew 5:3-16)

In modern-day theatrical musicals, the story often comes to a halt while the performers respond artistically to events of the plot with a song and a dance, enlightening the audience in an entertaining way. Like "Benjamin's Calypso," which breaks into *Joseph and the Amazing Technicolor Dreamcoat*, or "Marian the Librarian" in *The Music Man*, the Sermon on the Mount breaks into Matthew's narrative.

Although the synoptic Gospels (Matthew, Mark, and Luke) share a similar narrative of Jesus' life and ministry, Matthew's is unique in bringing the story line to a halt with five strategically placed discourses. These "sermons" enlighten readers by illustrating specific qualities of the kingdom of the heavens.[1] The narrative in Matthew could easily move along by going from 4:25 to 8:1b. But instead of only reporting that Jesus "went throughout Galilee, teaching in their synagogues and proclaiming the good news of the kingdom and curing every disease and every sickness among the people" (4:23), Matthew lets Jesus tell us in his own words why and how the kingdom of the heavens is good news. In so doing, as one commentator notes, Matthew allows his readers "to experience the breadth and power of Jesus' word" by presenting a whole sermon.[2]

How do we experience the word of Jesus, and in particular, this sermon? The Sermon on the Mount is often treated as a collection of parables and aphorisms of Jesus that add up to a revered list of rules for the Christian life. But if we accept his Sermon as a rule book, we do Jesus the injustice of forcing his teaching into the very trap he so passionately warns against: counting on the fulfilling of rules to be our ticket into the kingdom of the heavens. Time and again Jesus teaches that obeying the letter of the law does not fulfill righteousness. On the other hand, it is just as irresponsible for us to assume that this sermon is only the projection of an idealized, currently unattainable kingdom of God reserved for another age. In that case, we do the biblical text itself an injustice; we find ourselves selecting from the Bible what we will or will not accept as appropriate and applicable for our lives.

When Jesus announced, "Everybody change! The kingdom of the heavens is here!" (4:17 PKC), he meant now, this day. Most current English translations of Jesus' words say that the kingdom of the heavens "is near" or "at hand." Such a translation can give the impression that the kingdom is not necessarily here, but is available just around the corner. In his 1935 landmark study, *The Parables of the Kingdom*, C. H. Dodd argues that the original text shows more finality and that the arrival of the kingdom does not depend on our acceptance of it or on whether we change (repent). The kingdom is "a fact of present experience." The kingdom has arrived—it "has come."[3] In his own descriptive words, Jesus introduces that very kingdom to the common folk around him—and to us, Matthew's readers—and extends a generous welcome.

For many church people, the Beatitudes of Matthew 5:3-10 are as familiar as an everyday jacket and as welcome as a favorite meal. Many who grew up in Christian homes or attended Sunday school memorized them. I remember studying the Beatitudes in vacation Bible school as a child. We found it tough to decide what it meant to be meek and how to act that way in order to be good.

Can you imagine how many sermons over the centuries have been preached on the Beatitudes? Thousands and thousands, most likely. And with all that attention, they have been given many interpretations. Some people see them as law: obey them and you'll enter heaven. Some accept them as an impossible code of ethics to show how sinful we are and how much we need God's forgiving grace. Others say the unattainable, idealistic excellence of the Beatitudes does not apply to us here on earth but describes how things will be in heaven. Some believe the whole Sermon is only for the Jewish kingdom on earth.

We have been taught to pray, "Make us poor in spirit, O God" or "Make me meek," as if we are to seek those qualities in order to be blessed. We pray to be merciful, to be peacemakers, or even to mourn, so that by fulfilling those rules for living, we might become fit for heaven. But the Beatitudes are *de*scriptive of our situation, not *pre*scriptive. They acknowledge our condition, not what it needs to be. Jesus announces that the kingdom of the heavens welcomes us: the poor in spirit, those who mourn, the meek, those trying to find righteousness, those who are persecuted for the sake of righteousness. And it offers solace to those who show mercy, to those who have a pure heart, and to those who make peace. The list could go on. There is no limit to the kinds of people the kingdom welcomes, and no one is turned down because of his or her situation. Dallas Willard sums it up:

> The Beatitudes, in particular, are not teachings on *how* to be blessed. They are not instructions to do anything. . . . *They are explanations and illustrations, drawn from the immediate setting, of the present availability of the kingdom through personal relationship to Jesus.* They single out cases that provide proof that, in him, the rule of God from the heavens truly is available in life circumstances that are beyond all human hope.[4]

Ultimately it is a relief to know that you don't have to have all those special qualities to enter the kingdom. Who could? The Beatitudes are not a code of law to obey. And they certainly cannot be boiled down to our popular, mistaken, unscriptural motto, "God helps those who help themselves." It's really the opposite: God helps those who *can't* help themselves. Neither do you have to come from the religious elite to enter the kingdom of the heavens. It's for everyone. Besides, as Jesus points out later, considering ourselves the religious cream of the crop can actually work against us.

On first glance at the text, it is clear where the Beatitudes begin, but not where they end. Do they end with verse 10, or do they continue into verses 11 and 12? The text offers three clues. First, verses 3 through 10 are marked as a passage by the *inclusio* (the repetition of a word or phrase to mark a section), "for theirs is the kingdom of the heavens." Just as that phrase was used to finish the beatitude of verse 3, so it is used to finish the beatitude of verse 10, making those beatitudes a pair of bookends for the eight blessings. Second, the blessing that comes in verses 11 and 12 is longer than each of the previous eight blessings, causing a break in form. Third, the blessings of verses 3 through 10 refer to "those" and "theirs," whereas in verse 11 the listeners are addressed directly— "Blessed are you"—indicating a change. As we will see, verse 11 contains the first of several statements of direct address that give shape to the second part of Jesus' announcement.

For many years, as I recited the Beatitudes I used two syllables to pronounce the word *blessed*, and indeed, it is correctly said either as one or two syllables. Jesus is the Bless-ed One, the Son of God. But in the Beatitudes, my saying "bless-ed" served to confuse my understanding of what I now believe Jesus to be saying. To say "bless-ed" makes it sound as if the people themselves are holy, that they have achieved a state of blessedness by mourning, by being merciful, or by being hungry for righteousness—"Bless-ed are those who are persecuted for the sake of righteousness, for theirs is the kingdom of the heavens" (PKC). They appear to have earned their entrance into the kingdom. If, however, "bless-ed" is changed to one syllable (the alternate spelling, "blest," can be used), it suggests that the people are blessed with a gift of God, with grace—"Blest are the meek, for they will inherit the earth"—

not because they've earned it, but because it is given to them freely. The *New English Bible* captures some of that feeling:

> How blest are the sorrowful;
> > they shall find consolation. . . .
> How blest are those who show mercy;
> > mercy shall be shown to them (Matthew 5:4, 7).

Being blest is the opposite of being cursed. Jesus says, "You are blest because the kingdom is available to you, not cursed because you are an outcast among your neighbors." If people are poor in spirit or meek, or are longing to see the perfection of God, they should not consider that to be a curse. They should not feel as if they are "out of it" or on the bottom of the pile. They should consider themselves blest, says Jesus, for they are welcomed and cared for in the kingdom. The kingdom of God wants to befriend them.

People do not receive blessings because of who they are or what they do. They are blest because of what is available to them through the kingdom. Someone is not blessed by God *because* she is a peacemaker. And as we know, peacemakers are certain to be cursed by someone when they step into volatile, conflicted situations to bring about peace. That is the nature of the world we live in. But in the kingdom of the heavens, Jesus says, peacemakers will be called children of God, not meddling fools or cowards or yellow-bellied pacifists.

Over the years my wife, Nancy, has become a skilled quilter and has produced some beautiful, detailed work. As a Christmas gift one year I gave her a wall hanging that features a design of four quilt blocks. It declares: *Blessed are the PIECEmakers.* The gift was well received and certainly was given with love. A beatitude of that kind, however, can reinforce the common assumption that we are blessed because of the good things we do, that since Nancy is a quilter, she is blessed. It is true that in our everyday usage we commonly voice a thank-you by saying, "Blessings on you for teaching that Sunday school class." And there is nothing wrong with giving that kind of compliment; we all can use a blessing anytime. We also bless the Lord for all the goodness the Lord provides, which is a way of offering thanks. To think of the Beatitudes as teaching that we receive a blessing as a prize for our character or as a reward for something we've done is to misunderstand their meaning. Monika K. Hellwig offers a contrasting reminder.

> A blessing is a creative act; it brings something new into existence. It gives an increase of life and of the inheritance that God has bestowed upon his creatures. But a blessing is always expected to make the one who receives it the source of blessing for others; it is not expected to come to rest in its recipient and to end there. . . . Perhaps few Christians reflect that one is not blessed at the expense of others but for the benefit of others.[5]

The blessings of the beatitudes originate in the goodness of God and are manifest in the kingdom of the heavens. They are gifts of grace, blessings that come because of God's goodness, not because we deserve them, and they are designed to flow from God through us to those around us. I agree with Brenda, a friend of mine, who says she is "firmly convinced that one of the ways God communicates himself *to* us is *through* us." God made of Abram a great nation, and blessed him and made his name great, *so that he would be a blessing* (see Genesis 12:2).

In the text of Matthew 5:3-10, we notice that the outermost Beatitudes, the bookends, use the present tense ("theirs *is* the kingdom") and the inner six use the future tense ("for they *will*"). Not only do the first and eighth blessings identify themselves as the first and last of the Beatitudes, but they also give us a clue about how all eight might be understood. Let me put it this way: because the Beatitudes are enclosed by two blessings that use the phrase "for theirs is the kingdom of the heavens," all eight can be seen in the context of that phrase. It is within the kingdom that those who are pure in heart will see God and those who are hungry and thirsty for righteousness will be filled. Kingdom blessings come as a matter of course to all who are members of the kingdom. That is the benefit of being in the kingdom. That's how and where the meek inherit the earth, the merciful receive mercy, and the peacemakers are accepted for who they are—children of God.

It is in the community of the kingdom of the heavens that the blessings take place. As the righteousness of God is accepted and lived out within the purpose and standard of the kingdom, all the blessings of the kingdom are made manifest. The Beatitudes—and the entire Sermon on the Mount—are not to be understood as something for future reward but as describing the present fellowship of God's people living in mutual care and loving servanthood. Although God's kingdom awaits its full consummation on the day of the Lord, the kingdom of the heavens as Jesus presents it in Matthew begins to express the righteousness of God—now.

To put those observations into practice, let me add a few descriptive words to the text of the Beatitudes:

1. Blest are the poor in spirit, for [they live in] the kingdom of the heavens.
2. Blest are those who mourn, for they will be comforted [in the kingdom].
3. Blest are the meek, for they will inherit the earth [in the kingdom].
4. Blest are those who hunger and thirst for righteousness, for they will be filled [in the kingdom].
5. Blest are the merciful, for they will receive mercy [in the kingdom].
6. Blest are the pure in heart, for they will see God [in the kingdom].
7. Blest are the peacemakers, for they will be called children of God [in the kingdom].
8. Blest are those who are persecuted because of righteousness, for [they live in] the kingdom of the heavens.

Viewing the Beatitudes as being fulfilled in the kingdom may at first appear similar to their being received as prizes in heaven or in some other future age. But there is a big difference. The kingdom of the heavens is the present fellowship of God's people as established by Christ, not the faraway place we call heaven. As we discovered earlier, the kingdom of the heavens is both present and distant. It has no geographical boundaries or physical limits of space and time. When our earthly existence intersects with the heavenly realm, we enter the reality of the kingdom. It is not a figment of our imagination, nor is it limited by our human understanding. It is a divine gift as lavish as God's love in Christ and as powerful as the fellowship of the Holy Spirit. As his Sermon develops, Jesus expands on the description of life in the kingdom, and it becomes clear that blessings come as a present outgrowth of life experienced in the kingdom, not just as a reward in heaven.

"Welcome," Jesus proclaims, "God's kingdom is for you— all of you—now!"

But how can God's kingdom be available now? Does not the final day of the Lord signal the end of time when that kingdom comes? How does it come, and when? In the fifth discourse of Matthew, after Jesus predicts that all the stones of the temple will be thrown down, the disciples ask a similar question: "Tell us, when will these things be? And what will be the sign of your coming, and of the end of the age?" (24:3 NKJV). Jesus responds with a description of the days of turmoil to come for those who claim him as Lord. He tells how the Son of man will come on the clouds of heaven, sending out his angels to gather his elect from one end of the heavens to the other. Then he adds, "But of that day and hour no one knows, not even the angels of [the heavens], but My Father only" (24:36 NKJV).

Meanwhile, in the center of the sermon, Jesus teaches us to bring this request to God: "Your kingdom come. Your will be done, on earth as it is in heaven" (6:10). That appeal relates to now, not to some future time. It comes amid other examples of how to pray, all dealing with the present: give us bread for today, forgive us as we forgive, rescue us from the evil one. If the coming of God's kingdom suggests only the future end of earthly time, why does Jesus give us instructions in the Sermon on the Mount on how to live now? Why show us how to live spiritually, materially, and socially beyond the righteousness of the scribes and Pharisees? When Jesus was teaching in the synagogues, proclaiming the good news of the kingdom, and curing people of their illnesses (see Matthew 4:23-24), those ministries were signs that the kingdom of God was breaking into the present. In its *Confession of Faith*, Mennonite Church USA captures that perspective.

> We believe that God, who created the universe, continues to rule over it in wisdom, patience, and justice, though sinful creation has not yet recognized God's rule. Faithful Israel acclaimed God as king and looked forward to the fullness of God's kingdom. We affirm that, *in Jesus' ministry, death, and resurrection, the time of fulfillment has begun.* Jesus proclaimed both the nearness of God's reign and its future realization, its healing and its judgment. In his life and teaching, he showed that God's reign included the poor, outcasts, the persecuted, those who were like children, and those with faith like a mustard seed. For this kingdom, God has appointed Jesus Christ as king and Lord.
>
> We believe that *the church is called to live now according to the model of the future reign of God.* Thus, *we are given a foretaste* of the kingdom that God will one day establish in full. The church is to be a spiritual, social, and economic reality, *demonstrating now* the justice, righteousness, love, and peace of the age to come. *The church does this in obedience to its Lord and in anticipation that the kingdom of this world will become the kingdom of our Lord.* (italics added)[6]

With Fanny Crosby we sing, "Blessed assurance, Jesus is mine! Oh, what a foretaste of glory divine!"[7] and with William Mackay, "We praise thee, O God, for the joy thou hast giv'n to thy saints in communion, these foretastes of heav'n."[8] Both poets capture the "now, but not yet" character of God's kingdom, Crosby with the personal delight of faith in Christ and Mackay with the joy of Christ's community.

When we go to a banquet, we anticipate more than just the main course. As we gather, we informally greet each other while enjoying tasty hors d'oeuvres. There may be a formal, spoken welcome and an invitation to dine. Various courses of delicious foods are served while musicians perform. There may also be dinner theater or an after-dinner speech, followed by enticing desserts to top off the evening. Which part is the banquet? Do not all of these parts belong to the banquet? We cannot say that the hors d'oeuvres are not the banquet. Certainly they are not the full banquet, but neither is the main course. On the day of the Lord, the banquet will be complete. Now we have only a foretaste, but starting with the earthly life of Christ, the banquet has begun, even if only the savoring of hors d'oeuvres.

"Welcome," Jesus proclaims, "God's kingdom is for you— all of you—now!"

Immediately following the Beatitudes, Jesus becomes more direct: "You. *All of you* are blest when people abuse you on account of me" (5:11 PKC). Up to this point his announcement has been general—"they" and "those"—but now it becomes specific. Jesus still is addressing the people as a group, but becomes more personal than before. I can almost see Jesus making the switch from broad gesture and boisterous voice to a more focused tone. He may even get up and move from one to the other, standing face to face, looking people straight in the eye. It is true that God's word is always personal, that it always affects the individual, even when proclaimed in a general way. But there are times when all-embracing, foundational truth cuts like a knife through one's facade and touches personal reality. This is a time like that. And the group feels it. "Yes, you all are blest," Jesus says, "even when you all suffer abuse for me. Rejoice and be glad, all of you, for your reward is great in the heavens! You are being abused just like the prophets before you" (5:11-12 PKC).

Can this be right, the people ask? Is Jesus actually saying what we think he is saying? Is he telling us that we can be like the godly prophets of old, those who carried out God's will in the face of persecution? But it is our leaders, our religious leaders, who are persecuting us. Is his blessing on us a curse on them?

Jesus goes on. "It is you—the poor in spirit, the merciful, the meek, the pure in heart—who are the salt of the earth, not your leaders. My kingdom needs salt with flavor, not washed-out residue. It is you—those hungry for righteousness, the peacemakers, the persecuted, those who mourn—who are the light of the world, not your leaders. Celebrate your light! The world needs to see the kingdom of the heavens in all its glory. And when people see the good works of the kingdom taking place in you, they will praise the righteousness of your Father in the heavens" (5:13-16 PKC).

With a shudder the people say, "This is revolutionary." Such a vision of the kingdom of the heavens in all its glory was the focus of John the Baptist's prophecy (see Luke 3:4-6) and Mary's Magnificat (see Luke 1:49-53). Donald B. Kraybill writes,

> Paving the way for Jesus, the Baptist describes four surprises of the coming kingdom: full valleys, flat mountains, straight curves, and level bumps. He expects radical shake-ups in the new kingdom. Old ways will shatter beyond recognition. John warns us that the new order, the upside-down kingdom, will transform social patterns but amid the ferment, all flesh will see the salvation of God. . . .
>
> Mary expects the messianic kingdom to flip her social world upside down. The rich, mighty and

proud in Jerusalem will be banished. Poor farmers and shepherds in rural Galilee will be exalted and honored.[9]

In his move from generous welcome to direct address (5:11 and following), Jesus presents a capsule description of the kingdom's community structure. He tells the common people that together they can be like the prophets of old, who represented God in their day. God's righteousness, Jesus says, is not revealed through self-righteous religious leaders who self-importantly wallow in the heady hierarchy of their position. The kingdom of the heavens does not welcome oppression, whatever its source. Instead it nurtures a mutual community of God's love shared by people from every walk of life. God's kingdom offers freedom and acceptance for everyone, not just for leaders or for those who appear to be important.

If we think such a message surprised Jesus' contemporaries, his truth has an even more fresh—and radical—ring to it for us in the twenty-first century. But why should we be surprised? That has been the word of God from the beginning. Here Jesus merely picks up and restates a foundational theme already expressed in the Hebrew scriptures as far back as the creation story. And after the ascension that same theme will be carried on by the writers of the New Testament—that God endows every Christian believer with grace-gifts (charismata) and that every person is granted the courtesy of being heard.[10]

The ancient, powerful narrative preserved for us in Numbers 11 affirms God's intention that mutual responsibility and divine anointing be distributed among the people. God has instructed Moses to gather seventy leaders of Israel at the tabernacle so God can take some of the Spirit that is on Moses and put it on the others. At the time this takes place, two of the seventy leaders, Eldad and Medad, are not at the tabernacle, but are still at the camp. So when the Lord comes down and puts the Spirit on the sixty-eight, and they prophesy, so do Eldad and Medad at the camp.

> A young man ran and reported to Moses, "Eldad and
> Medad are prophesying in the camp!" Joshua son of
> Nun, who had been Moses' personal assistant since
> his youth, protested, "Moses, my master, make them
> stop!" But Moses replied, "Are you jealous for my
> sake? I wish that all the Lord's people were prophets,
> and that the Lord would put his Spirit upon them all!"
> (Numbers 11:27-29 NLT)

Jesus says that people in the kingdom are like the
prophets of old. The prophets were God's representatives and
so are kingdom people. As Moses had passionately envisioned, everyone in the kingdom receives the divine Spirit.
Everyone together makes up the kingdom, not just leaders.
Jesus tells the people, "Don't be sad or confused if you are
persecuted on my account. So were the prophets. Instead,
shout for joy! Be glad! Because your reward is great in the
heavens—now! Not sometime in the future. Now—in the
kingdom of the heavens" (5:11-12 PKC).

The concept of reward shows up several times in the
Sermon on the Mount, and we will discuss it more fully
later.[11] I tend to think of "reward" in a selfish way, as something that praises me for doing something well or for doing a
good thing. Rewards are prizes offered for such things as giving information that leads to finding a lost dog or catching a
thief. I remember being rewarded with a little flashlight by
my father for getting all my chores done and practicing my
piano lesson before suppertime. Pastor Firman Gingerich
told us in his story that if he did well in school and did his
chores at home, he got to go to town with his dad on
Saturday and would get a stick of licorice at the store and a
book from the library. Rewards always imply a consequence,
whether good or bad, and there is nothing wrong in wisely
using rewards as incentives.

But Jesus is not saying that when kingdom people receive
persecution, we should rejoice because by and by we will get

jewels in our crowns for good behavior. He is not saying that a great reward awaits us in heaven. He is saying that our reward is great *in the heavens*. When disciples manifest the gracious life of Christ in the kingdom of the heavens, the reward is already there. Although people may receive persecution on account of Christ, the kingdom always extends the comfort, solace, and delight of God's righteousness—a reward of mutual care that is spiritually, materially, and socially life-giving. Kingdom people need not, and should not, let a seeming setback like nasty persecution by this world overwhelm their life together. Even in the extreme case of death by martyrdom for Christ, the martyr is ushered into the full presence of God. Rejoice and be glad! When one is a member of the kingdom, that in itself becomes the satisfying and bounteous reward. The abundant life of Christ is always present in the kingdom of the heavens, demonstrated by generous mutuality and joy.

On the night before his crucifixion, Jesus visualized that very community of righteousness in his "high priestly prayer." Fervently setting forth his vision, Jesus gladly acknowledges that he has been glorified—made visible—in those disciples whom he has called, taught, and loved, and he sees that very manifestation as continuing into the future (see John 17:20-23). Jesus prays to his Father about his disciples:

> Everything mine is yours, and yours mine,
> And my life is on display in them.
> For I'm no longer going to be visible in the world;
> They'll continue in the world
> While I return to you.
> Holy Father, guard them as they pursue this life
> That you conferred as a gift through me,
> So they can be one heart and mind
> As we are one heart and mind. (John 17:10-11 Msg)

"Welcome," Jesus proclaims, "God's kingdom is for you—all of you—now! And that kingdom is God's community of righteousness."

For Discussion

Blessings are creative acts that do not come to rest in the ones receiving them, but find their completion in becoming the source of blessing for others. The Beatitudes describe abundant blessings that tell of life in the kingdom of the heavens. Create similar beatitudes for everyday kingdom life around you. For example, "Blest are pastors who diligently prepare and preach weekly sermons, for they will be heard with gratitude." Or, "Blest are those who sacrifice to keep the local food pantry shelves stocked, for they also will have plenty to eat."

Here's an eye-opening reminder by John Andrew Holmes, American physician and writer of the early twentieth century: "It is well to remember that the entire universe, with one trifling exception, is composed of others." Relate his observation to life in the kingdom of the heavens.

Jesus tells his listeners that others will see their good works and give glory to their Father in the heavens (see Matthew 5:16). We often shy away from the phrase "good works," especially when referring to our Christian life. But Paul writes in Ephesians 2:10 that Christians are those who are "created in Christ Jesus for good works, which God prepared beforehand to be our way of life." Describe those good works.

— 4 —

Law Is Law
Why Is That Not Enough?

Do not think that I have come to abolish the law or the prophets; I have come not to abolish but to fulfill. For truly I tell you, until heaven and earth pass away, not one letter, not one stroke of a letter, will pass from the law until all is accomplished. Therefore, whoever breaks one of the least of these commandments, and teaches others to do the same, will be called least in the kingdom of [the heavens]; but whoever does them and teaches them will be called great in the kingdom of [the heavens]. For I tell you, unless your righteousness exceeds that of the scribes and Pharisees, you will never enter the kingdom of [the heavens].

You have heard that it was said to those of ancient times, "You shall not murder"; and "whoever murders shall be liable to judgment." But I say to you that if you are angry with a brother or sister, you will be liable to judgment; and if you insult a brother or sister, you will be liable to the council; and if you say, "You fool," you will be liable to the hell of fire. So when you are offering your gift at the altar, if you remember that your brother or sister has something against you, leave your gift there before the altar and go; first be reconciled to your brother or sister, and then come and offer your gift. Come to terms quickly with your accuser while you are on the way to court with him, or your accuser may hand you over to the judge, and the judge to the guard, and you will be thrown into prison. Truly I tell you, you will never get out until you have paid the last penny.

You have heard that it was said, "You shall not commit adultery." But I say to you that everyone who looks at a woman with lust has already committed adultery with her in his heart. If your right eye causes you to sin, tear it out and throw it away; it is better for you to lose one of your members than for your whole body to be thrown into hell. And if your right hand causes you to sin, cut it off and throw it away; it is better for you to lose one of your members than for your whole body to go into hell.

It was also said, "Whoever divorces his wife, let him give her a certificate of divorce." But I say to you that anyone who divorces his wife, except on the ground of unchastity, causes her to commit adultery; and whoever marries a divorced woman commits adultery. (Matthew 5:17-32)

There are times—tragic times—when things spin out of control. We'd like to go back and do things differently, but we can't. U.S. Representative Bill Janklow, a dominating figure in South Dakota politics for nearly thirty years, found himself in such a spot.

Jurors in the congressman's boyhood hometown convicted Janklow of second-degree manslaughter, reckless driving, running a stop sign and speeding for the Aug. 16 [2003] crash that killed Randy Scott, 55, a farmer from Hardwick, Minn. Prosecutors said Janklow was traveling more than 70 mph in a white Cadillac when he crashed with Scott's Harley-Davidson.[1]

Janklow indicated he would resign from Congress the following January, when he was scheduled to be sentenced, saying he would be "unable to perform the duties incumbent on me in representing the people of South Dakota as their U.S. representative." The previous year he had been elected to the state's lone House seat after serving sixteen years as governor, which followed four earlier years as attorney general. Janklow won over legions of voters in heavily conservative South Dakota with his tough-talking, maverick style. He received numerous speeding tickets and was an unapologetic speeder, as he revealed during a 1999 speech to the Legislature: "Bill Janklow speeds when he drives—shouldn't, but he does," Janklow said then. "When he gets the ticket he pays it, but if someone told me I was going to jail for two days for speeding, my driving habits would change."

How sad that Janklow's bravura turned sour, bringing a disgraceful end to his career and snuffing out Scott's life. His unhappy tale is repeated here not to bring shame on anyone but to illustrate how casually all of us can treat the everyday laws of our land. Negligence of the law is common, and many of us find ourselves in Janklow's shoes. But because he was well known, it is Janklow himself who drew attention to the deadly consequences of his careless driving and insensitivity to the law, even though his profession is built on the law.

We need to ask what it means to obey the law and what it means to live in such a way that our life expresses the "righteousness" that flows from beyond the law. To do that we need to look further at Jesus' Sermon on the Mount.

When Jesus announced that the community of the kingdom of the heavens welcomes people from all walks of life, he knew he would get a positive response. When he declared that God's kingdom offers freedom and acceptance for everyone, not just for leaders, he knew it would sound radical. He knew people would sense the breaking down of law and the makings of a revolution. But he was ready. He turned to them with a slight reprimand: "Don't misunderstand why I have come. I did not come to abolish the law of Moses or the writings of the prophets. No, I came to fulfill them" (Matthew 5:17 NLT).

The people were stunned. Wait a minute, they said. They had begun drooling with imagined, newfound power. They were on the verge of insurrection. They were tired of second-class citizenship and had been waiting too long already for a messiah who would lead them in a takeover. The burden of law was heavy. "Religious stuff" was being pushed down their throats. They wanted no more oppression from the hierarchy.

Did Jesus say he did not come to abolish the law? Did he say he came to fulfill it? Is Jesus using double-talk? How can he announce the formation of such an upside-down kingdom and then go back on his word? But Jesus will show that God's will and purpose never change. "Not one letter, not one stroke of a letter will pass from the law" (5:18). God's law is always law, and always right. It is when law is abused by conniving leaders and turned toward selfish ends that the law itself appears to be bad and causes problems for those who are being oppressed. In his later ministry, Jesus dealt directly with that kind of disobedience.

> The scribes and the Pharisees sit on Moses' seat; therefore, do whatever they teach you and follow it; but do not do as they do, for they do not practice what they teach. They tie up heavy burdens, hard to bear, and lay them on the shoulders of others; but they themselves are unwilling to lift a finger to move them. (Matthew 23:1-4)

Such offensive behavior is compounded if those same experts in the law and other religious leaders appear to be in collusion with the rulers from Rome. So while the scribes and Pharisees are making the law work in their favor, the common people are struggling for existence. No wonder they want out—from under the law and from under their leaders.

When Jesus cites the law and the prophets, he is referring to the pillars of Israel's faith. "The law" is the five books of Moses (the Pentateuch), and "the prophets" the rest of the Hebrew scriptures. As Gospel writer Luke shows in Jesus' interaction with the disciples on the road to Emmaus, this was familiar territory for Jesus: "Then, starting with Moses and going through all the prophets, he explained to them the passages throughout the scriptures that were about himself (24:27 NJB).

It is easy to comprehend the Jewish love for the law, according to Daniel J. Harrington.

> The English term "Law" can distort the Jewish understanding of Torah. The word "Torah" derives from the Hebrew verb "instruct" (*yrh*) and refers to the teaching or instruction presented in the Scriptures, especially the Pentateuch. For Jews the Torah was (and is) the revelation of God's will, a kind of divine blueprint for action. It is a gift and a privilege given to Israel, not a burden.[2]

Jesus came to restore God's gift and privilege! As his hearers in the first and twenty-first centuries come to see, it is precisely on his point of fulfilling God's divine blueprint that Jesus establishes God's righteousness as the law of the kingdom of the heavens. After his resurrection, Jesus told his followers, "This is what I meant by saying, while I was still with you, that everything written about me in the Law of Moses and in the prophets and psalms was bound to be fulfilled" (Luke 24:44 NEB). My mission, Jesus says, is to fulfill God's law of righteousness—through my human birth, ministry, suffering, death, and resurrection. Now the kingdom community will put God's righteousness into practice as it proclaims repentance and forgiveness of sins to all nations. The community is the witness of these things! And for this divine task the community will be clothed with power from on high (see Luke 24:45-49).

In the Sermon on the Mount Jesus spells out this very law of righteousness, identified by another use of the literary device *inclusio*. In 5:17 he says, "I did not come to abolish *the law or the prophets*." Then in 7:12 he says, "for this is *the law and the prophets*." These bookends establish the beginning and end of the remarkable core of Jesus' unsurpassed sermon, in which he teaches the validity, meaning, and practical application of God's law.

In 5:19 Jesus begins his sobering put-down of self-important religious leaders. He declares that those who parade their false superiority in the law as righteousness will be judged by every bit of the law. So beware. All those, especially the experts in the law, who break even a minuscule part of the law and teach others their clever loopholes, will be seen as the least, not the greatest, in the kingdom (consider the sad story of Janklow). It is the ones who put the law into practice—who truly value the law and teach it to others—who will be called great in the kingdom of the heavens. Those who grasp for greatness in the kingdom, Jesus says, will not acquire it. That's impossible.

In Matthew 18, the fourth discourse is introduced by disciples who come to Jesus with an important question on this matter and, I suspect, with smugness on their faces. They ask, "Who is the greatest in the kingdom of the heavens?" Jesus puts a child in their midst and says, "Truly I tell you, unless you change and become like little children, you will never enter the kingdom of [the heavens]. Therefore, whoever takes a humble place—becoming like this child—is the greatest in the kingdom of [the heavens]" (verses 3-4 TNIV).

If humility identifies one as being the greatest in the kingdom, it truly is impossible to achieve greatness by scheming to be the greatest. For those who search for greatness in the kingdom, it is impossible to actually achieve that goal. Anyone lording it over others certainly cannot attain greatness, since it is the humble who are the greatest. Try teaching that to us in North America.

Philippians 3 records the testimony of a formerly self-righteous church leader. The apostle Paul tells it like it is. No more does he boast about his status or count on it for greatness. That's all changed.

> If others think they have reasons to put confidence in
> the flesh, I have more: circumcised on the eighth day,
> of the people of Israel, of the tribe of Benjamin, a

Hebrew of Hebrews; in regard to the law, a Pharisee; as for zeal, persecuting the church; as for righteousness based on the law, faultless.

But whatever were gains to me I now consider loss for the sake of Christ. What is more, I consider everything a loss because of the surpassing worth of knowing Christ Jesus my Lord, for whose sake I have lost all things. I consider them garbage, that I may gain Christ and be found in him, not having a righteousness of my own that comes from the law, but that which is through faith in Christ—the righteousness that comes from God on the basis of faith. I want to know Christ—yes, to know the power of his resurrection and participation in his sufferings, becoming like him in his death, and so, somehow, attaining to the resurrection from the dead. (Philippians 3:4-11 TNIV)

Paul caught the vision of Jesus and discarded earned "righteousness" in the pharisaical system to gain membership among the brothers and sisters of the kingdom created anew in Christ Jesus. In Matthew 5:17-20 Jesus' pronouncement is twofold. First, the new community that values common people and accepts their involvement in mutual leadership is built on God's righteous law, not on our law or anybody else's. Second, the offensive, deceptive understanding of kingdom righteousness that has become the norm for the scribes and Pharisees has got to go. Such false leaders are like musicians who show off their performance technique but lack the truth of the music. John Fischer writes, "Righteousness for the Pharisees was a system, not an inner reality. It was external, not internal. It was, from beginning to end, a calculated manipulation of the law that awarded them technical righteousness, albeit through a cold heart."[3]

Righteousness from God wants to flow throughout the daily life of the kingdom and be made visible by the lives of all who participate. It is not to be squelched by any who see themselves as more important than the community or any of its individual members. Besides, no one should try to beat the scribes and Pharisees at their own game of trying to gain righteousness with a perfect scorecard. Even though we may try, we are unable to compete at their level of rules-keeping. Jesus makes it clear: "For I tell you, unless your righteousness goes beyond that of the experts in the law and the Pharisees, you will never enter the kingdom of [the heavens]" (5:20 NET). To go beyond the righteousness of the scribes and Pharisees is not a directive to surpass them at keeping the rules of righteousness technically, but to live beyond those laws. It is the call for a change of heart so that all of life will flow from righteousness; only the cold heart claims righteousness as a reward for keeping the law. Keeping the law does not come from following a rule book, but from being in the presence of the source of righteousness. That way God's righteousness flows out as naturally as the stream follows the watercourse. The doxology has it right: "Praise God from whom all blessings flow."

To interpret God's law of righteousness, Jesus puts forward six laws that are well known. Those laws—concerning murder, adultery, divorce, oaths, retaliation, prejudice—are not ones that anyone would argue against. Everyone knows them as law. In fact, the religious leaders are well acquainted with them because of manipulating and massaging them for their own gain. So it is not because Jesus chooses to speak about those specific laws that people are on the edge of their seats. It's what he does with them. Six times, with only slight variation, Jesus says, "You have heard that it was said," then immediately follows the law with "but." And with every "but" he sends a shiver through the crowd. Every "but" is an alert that all who are misunderstanding God's law and misusing its technicalities to their advantage need to listen up, as Thomas G. Long, in his commentary on Hebrews, notes.

> Every sermon listener knows that the little conjunction "but" is a dagger, swiftly attacking whatever

stands before in favor of what is about to come, a trumpet heralding the appearance of something unprecedented. The word "but" is a rhetorical clue that what the Preacher has just been saying, indeed what the hearers have been taking in without question, is about to fall under challenge. Something new is about to emerge to rival the old, and the language of contrast forms a familiar biblical pattern.[4]

With that one little word, Jesus is indeed preaching something new. As he moves through the examples, it becomes apparent that his concern is about fulfilling the spirit of the law, not its rigid technicalities.

The first ancient law Jesus chooses is clear: "You shall not murder" and "whoever murders shall be liable to judgment" (see Exodus 20:13; Deuteronomy 5:17-21). If I followed the letter of the law, I would not take anyone's life, and I would be righteous legally. Justice would be served. But if I acted out my anger on someone, carefully following the precise detail of the command, it would mean that I could beat someone to within an inch of his life but not kill him, and that would be acceptable and legal. Or in similar fashion, what would keep me legally from physically abusing someone so she could no longer walk or talk? If I didn't kill her, I'd be within the law.

The only legal way to cover both situations would be to make more laws: You shall not beat a person to within an inch of his life; you shall not abuse a person so she cannot walk or talk. But how severely would I be allowed to beat or maim someone and still do it legally? A little? A lot? What constitutes a little or a lot? So how many rules would it take to cover those situations?

One summer while playing miniature golf with Alex, my grandson, I picked up this list of rules:
1. Play at your own risk.
2. No smoking or alcohol permitted on the premises.

3. Stay on the sidewalks and fairways **at all times**.
4. Do not climb on rocks or ropes.
5. Do not swing putter above knees.
6. Do not strike any object other than golf ball with putter.

Failure to comply with the rules will result in your removal from the premises. No refunds.

Those rules are understandable and helpful, but even so, they do not cover all kinds of conduct. How is one to treat people playing ahead of you or behind you? Nothing is said about how you are to dress, about loud talk or profanity, or about whether you can play your boom box. And what about gross behavior such as chewing a wad of tobacco and spitting on the sidewalks and fairways? If we are to live by rules, there needs be a rule for every possible situation in life.

We can imagine why the Pharisees built up such a long list. We try this too. Have you studied recently to take the written test for a new driver's license? Or do you struggle with IRS tax forms each year? Even with all the laws on the books—from community ordinances to financial regulations to international travel—we still find loopholes. Laws are not enough. And it becomes obvious that we need something more than law to guide our lives.

Jesus is pointing out that our hearts are devious and that our whole life experience needs a center of authenticity other than law so we can live as God intended. When our living is centered on God's goodness, the rule of righteousness is fulfilled. When we live by our own standards, evil is inevitable. But we have a choice, because God created us with the capability to choose. God created us to live in God's goodness, rightness, and beauty. When we choose our own way, our selfishness ruins that design. So in God's love, Jesus offers the kingdom of the heavens as a re-creation of life as it was in the garden of Eden, where life flows out from God and rules are not needed, except for one: live by God's righteousness, not by your own knowledge and wisdom.

When the woman came to me and asked what my church allowed, she probably was seeking to know either how to become righteous or how irresponsibly she could live and still remain righteous. In the six examples of Matthew 5:21-48, Jesus shows that there is only one law: God's law of righteousness. The laws he cites, along with innumerable laws not listed there, all can be covered by living according to God's goodness and love. In a revealing way, such living conforms to the biblical view that love covers a multitude of sins (Proverbs 10:12; 1 Peter 4:8).

Jesus says that when the law about not murdering is seen in light of God's law of righteousness, it means more than fulfilling the technical detail of actually not murdering someone. Anyone who gets angry with a brother or sister, insults someone, or says to someone, "You fool," has broken God's law. That is much broader than the single act of killing someone; it puts the responsibility on every person to live in God's goodness. The urge to kill actually grows out of anger that is not dealt with appropriately. Richard B. Gardner writes, "In all of this, Jesus' point is not that his hearers should revise the legal code to punish hate and anger. His intent is, instead, to show that every act or emotion that threatens life in one's community violates God's will."[5]

Jesus said that if you build up anger at someone, you are breaking the law of "do not murder." To live God's law of righteousness means to make things right with others so that anger is dissolved and does not lead to murder. One could even say that being unduly angry with someone is a kind of murder, since we elevate ourselves above the other person with an arrogance that refuses to recognize the humanity of the other. We do that in war, calling our enemies savages or evil. We do not allow them to exist as persons—on our level, at least.

Anger arises not only from us against others, but others get angry at us too for our offenses against them (see Matthew 5:23-26). Deal with that kind of discord person to person, Jesus says. Find peace with whoever is angry with you, or the community will suffer. If I cause someone to resort to a court's ruling, just so she can find some kind of resolution to an offense I have caused, I have created a serious breach in community. When that happens, Jesus says, my worship cannot be genuine. I must go and make things right with others so we can worship, and so I can come into, or stay within, the presence of the one who is holy and righteous. The ancient poetry of the psalmist says it this way:

> Who shall ascend the hill of the LORD? And who shall stand in his holy place? Those who have clean hands and pure hearts, who do not lift up their souls to what is false, and do not swear deceitfully. They will receive blessing from the LORD, and vindication from the God of their salvation. (Psalm 24:3-5)

In 5:27-30 Jesus continues his interpretation of God's kingdom righteousness by selecting a law on committing adultery (see Exodus 20:14; Deuteronomy 5:18). Here again, breaking the law is not based only on the actual technicality of committing the crime, but also on what causes the infraction. When your lust, your desire to sin, has invaded your thinking and you are sensing the fulfillment of the possibilities, you have already gone too far. Cleansing at God's throne is needed. Even if you were caught in the act of adultery, and you were able to finagle a decision of legal justice from the civil court, never would that settlement stand up as satisfying the rule of God's righteousness. The kingdom of the heavens operates out of love and respect for each other as God's children, and if you have trouble with living like that, you might as well poke out your eye or tear off your hand to keep yourself in line.

When Jesus speaks of the eye or the hand that "causes you to sin" (or "causes you to stumble" or "offends you"), the Greek word he uses is the one that gives the English language its word *scandal*. In that case, the phrase would read literally, "if your right eye (or hand) scandalizes you." In the third discourse, one of the parables about the kingdom of the heavens concerns the weeds of the field (see Matthew 13:24-30, followed by Jesus' explanation in verses 36-43). At the end of the age, Jesus says, the Son of man will send his angels to his kingdom where they will collect and burn the weeds, which include "all scandalous things and those breaking the law" (41-42 PKC). In contrast, when the weeds are removed from the fields, "then the righteous will shine like the sun in the kingdom of their Father" (verse 43 PKC). Here in the Sermon on the Mount (5:29-30), Jesus takes care to spell out the difference between being scandalous and being righteous. And as he says in Matthew 13, the righteous will shine like the sun, but the alternative is disastrous.

Without stopping, Jesus moves directly from redefining adultery to a law on divorce in Deuteronomy 24:1-4: "Whoever divorces his wife, let him give her a certificate of divorce" (5:31-32). It is a quick transition, and George R. Ewald comments,

> One could paraphrase [verse 31]: "While I'm on the topic of adultery, what about the man who puts away his wife with the excuse of a divorce bill?" In this passage Jesus is not as concerned about a man divorcing an unfaithful spouse as he is with the irresponsible divorce because of the selfishness of the male. He challenges the previously undisputed power of the husband's patriarchal right.[6]

Chapter 19 of Matthew's Gospel gives a helpful perspective. There some Pharisees come to test Jesus with a question concerning this very law: "Is it lawful for a man to divorce his wife for any cause?" (verse 3). When Jesus responds that no one should separate what God has joined together, the Pharisees push on, seeking to prove him wrong: "Why then did Moses command us to give a certificate of dismissal and to divorce her?" But Jesus turns their "proof" back on them, saying, "It was because you were so hard-hearted that Moses allowed you to divorce your wives" (verse 7-8). Ouch! Then in the same breath Jesus adds a phrase that speaks not only to them but also to the underlying focus in his Sermon. He states frankly, "But from the beginning it was not so" (verse 8). "The beginning" Jesus refers to is the garden of Eden, where humankind was created male and female (verse 4; see also Genesis 1:27) and where they marry and "become one flesh" (verse 5; see also Genesis 2:24). Jesus said that discussion of divorce and remarriage must be put in the framework of God's intention for marriage. The original plans did not include provision or regulations for divorce. Consequently Jesus did not say, "You can't divorce" but "Don't divorce." Men should stop doing what they were doing for selfish reasons: tearing apart what God had put together. The bottom line, Jesus says, is that they were not to use the legal option of divorce papers for improper reasons outside the law of righteousness.

It is clear that selfish desires lead to our trying to live above the law, exploiting the rules for our benefit. Instead, kingdom values as Jesus interprets them look beyond the law to the goodness of God. Obeying rules—even good ones—does not make one a Christian. If it did, how many of us could attain to being Christian? Like Pastor Firman Gingerich, we would keep trying "harder and harder and harder." And like Bill Janklow, we would come to a sad time when we'd have to eat our words. Knowing we need help to conform to God's goodness, Jesus does not let up. He pushes even further into the scope of God's righteousness as he interprets the fourth, fifth, and sixth laws.

For Discussion

Vince Lombardi, legendary coach of the Green Bay Packers, is supposed to have said, "Winning isn't everything—it's the only thing." That philosophy may work in professional football, but is it something for everyday life? How does such an attitude compare with life in the kingdom of the heavens?

In Clue, Romania, Andrei Dombi, an ethnic Hungarian with dual Romanian and French citizenship, thought he was married to Anca Diana Toma after he said yes in Hungarian, Romanian, and French—*igen, da, oui.* But the civil servant who performed marriages refused to marry the couple because the groom was supposed to give his consent first in the Romanian language. The couple said they would sue.[7] If you had been the civil servant, what would you have done? When is law law, and how is law to be treated? What "law is law" situations have you experienced?

A friend told me this story, which had taken place at a church before he became its pastor: A woman had given birth to a child out of wedlock. Later she met and married a man from that church and they raised a number of children. But they developed no relationship with the church. After a number of years, she and her husband had a faith experience that transformed their lives. Riding on that wave of newfound spiritual commitment, they began bringing their whole family to attend the husband's former church and felt led to renew their marriage vows as Christians. When they asked the pastor to officiate their renewal, he refused because her first child had been born out of wedlock. If you had been their pastor, would you have officiated their renewal? And how would your congregation react?

— 5 —

Code of Conduct
I'm Only Protecting My Interests

Again, you have heard that it was said to those of ancient times, "You shall not swear falsely, but carry out the vows you have made to the Lord." But I say to you, Do not swear at all, either by heaven, for it is the throne of God, or by the earth, for it is his footstool, or by Jerusalem, for it is the city of the great King. And do not swear by your head, for you cannot make one hair white or black. Let your word be "Yes, Yes" or "No, No"; anything more than this comes from the evil one.

You have heard that it was said, "An eye for an eye and a tooth for a tooth." But I say to you, Do not resist an evildoer. But if anyone strikes you on the right cheek, turn the other also; and if anyone wants to sue you and take your coat, give your cloak as well; and if anyone forces you to go one mile, go also the second mile. Give to everyone who begs from you, and do not refuse anyone who wants to borrow from you.

You have heard that it was said, "You shall love your neighbor and hate your enemy." But I say to you, Love your enemies and pray for those who persecute you, so that you may be children of your Father in [the heavens]; for he makes his sun rise on the evil and on the good, and sends rain on the righteous and on the unrighteous. For if you love those who love you, what reward do you have? Do not even the tax collectors do the same? And if you greet only your brothers and sisters, what more are you doing than others? Do not even the Gentiles do the same? Be perfect, therefore, as your heavenly Father is perfect. (Matthew 5:33-48)

On April 17, 1992, Terry Waite was interviewed by Barbara Walters on ABC TV's *20/20*. Waite had represented the Church of England in negotiations to try to win the release of Americans who were being held hostage in the Middle East. On that mission in 1987, Waite himself was kidnapped and held hostage, and was released shortly before the *20/20* interview. Walters asked, "Did you ever try to escape?"

Waite: I didn't. I had an opportunity, but I didn't take it.
Walters: Why?
Waite: Well, it's this. I'd argued with the guards—with the kidnappers, I beg your pardon. Long before I was kidnapped, I used to say to them, "It's absolutely futile for you to keep engaging in violence and violent activities. It's self-defeating. Give it up. Use your brains. Renounce violence." And then, one day, when I was captured, when I was a hostage, I asked to go to the bathroom. There was just one guard in the room at the time and he unpadlocked me, unpadlocked my feet and my hands—it was a time when I was chained up completely. And I got into the bathroom and took my blindfold off—the door was closed—and I discovered on top of the cistern an automatic weapon. I looked at it and it was loaded and I concluded that he'd left it there mistakenly. I thought, "Here's a chance," and then, immediately, I said to myself, "Well, what have you been saying? You've been saying to these men, 'When you're in a tight corner, renounce violence.'" And now, here was I in a tight corner and was I going to use violence? Because if I'd picked up that gun, I'd have had to use it. I'd have had to hurt someone. I thought, "No. I must stand by what I believe." And so I knocked on the door—put

my blindfold back on, knocked on the door and said,
"Take it. I want nothing more to do with it."[1]

Walters went on to ask Waite if he was "bucking for
sainthood," but he replied that he was only standing by what
he believed and had declared. If Waite had taken the gun and
fought his way out, he would have been hailed as a hero.
Current thinking among most people would be to protect
oneself, taking every means to escape, even if violence was
involved. Popular opinion, and probably the law, would say
that Waite had every lawful right to defend himself and to
escape. But he didn't escape. I commend him for what he
actually did in the power of God's Spirit.

Jesus is dealing in his Sermon with that kind of kingdom
attribute. As he moves on to introduce the fourth law, he
adds a one-word connection and reiterates a brief phrase
from the beginning of his interpretation (5:21): "*Again*, you
have heard that it was said *to those of ancient times*" (verse
33, italics added). In a subtle way, those additions to the pattern indicate a slight change and development in the discussion. In commenting on the first three laws, Jesus had spoken
of relationships within the familiar proximity of family and
close neighbors, although murder certainly can have a broader context. In this second set of three laws, he expands his
interpretation into a more general arena. By selecting laws
four, five, and six for interpretive discussion, Jesus begins to
fill out what he had referred to earlier in his Sermon when he
compared the life of the kingdom of the heavens to being a
lamp that floods light on all people:

> If I make you light-bearers, you don't think I'm going
> to hide you under a bucket, do you? I'm putting you
> on a light stand. Now that I've put you there on a hill-
> top, on a light stand—shine! Keep open house; be gen-
> erous with your lives. By opening up to others, you'll
> prompt people to open up with God, this generous
> Father in [the heavens]. (5:15-16 Msg)

Jesus presses on to a law on integrity, quoting Leviticus 19:12: "You shall not swear falsely, but carry out the vows you have made to the Lord" (verse 33). The law is about candidly telling the truth, about my doing what I said I would do. It's about living up to my commitment to God and Christ's kingdom. It's about living honestly among my neighbors and community so that everyone with whom I interact can put faith in me. As my late father, a pastor, would say to the congregation, "I want to be transparent before you." What Jesus is getting at here is our sinful inclination to put a false front on things, whether we are leaders or followers. No matter how well we dress up a lie, it is still a lie. No matter how many Sundays in a row I participate in worship, my shady business dealings during the week are still wrong. No matter what attractive public image a "Christian" family portrays, any abuse that goes on behind drawn shades cannot be justified. To bring God into the picture as confirmation of our character does not make evil good.

This fourth law brings to mind the fickle pledge children sometimes make: "I cross my heart and hope to die." And it directly relates to putting a hand on the Bible and answering the question, "Do you swear to tell the truth, the whole truth, and nothing but the truth, so help you God?" Naming God as supportive collateral is like playing a trump card. Even when our word is false, we might swear that it's true, just to prove our point.

Being completely honest can be tough. In the January 14, 2001, *New York Times*, Linda Holland describes her thoughts at the time she listed her 1988 Saab for sale on the Internet: "Nothing tests your ethics like selling a used car."[2] In the public arena, political figures accused of engaging in something illegal or promiscuous often hotly protest, "I categorically deny it!" At that I cynically conclude, "They're guilty." As Shakespeare's Queen Gertrude suggests to her son, Hamlet, "The lady doth protest too much, methinks."

In Leviticus 19 the law about not swearing falsely is found among a list of regulations on how to deal uprightly with others. That chapter itself is part of a larger group of laws sometimes called the Holiness Code (Leviticus 17—26) because of its central theme: "Be holy because I, the LORD your God, am holy" (Leviticus 19:2 TNIV). Holiness comes from God, who is holy, not from those whom God has chosen. It is instructive that Jesus chooses the fourth, fifth, and sixth laws directly from the Holiness Code. Might his use of them be a clue that living in the presence of the holy God is the way for the kingdom of the heavens to let its light shine? As for the law about not swearing falsely, regulations that surround it in Leviticus 19 include ordinances about gleanings from the harvest, stealing, exploitation, withholding wages, favoritism, and gossip. If the rule on not swearing falsely is taken in context, its essence clearly deals with more than just telling a lie. So if the fulfillment of the law of God's righteousness is to be an everyday reality, members of the kingdom of the heavens will need to live transparent lives: what people see is what they get; what happens Sunday morning is what happens during the week. Jesus says, "You're not in the same league as God who made heaven and earth, so don't act like you are. You really can't make your hair white or black, even though you try. It's all false. Just say yes or no, and live up to it. If you try to prove your point by any other means, you are flirting with evil instead of good" (5:34-37 PKC).

Moving on to the fifth law—do not resist an evildoer (verses 38-42)—Jesus gets too close for comfort. He's in my face. I do think I can work to control my anger, and I can understand what Jesus means about adultery and divorce. And I've always tried to be what I'd call an honest person. But now is he really asking me not to resist an evildoer? Am I supposed to let anybody do to me whatever they want, and accept it? I like the old way better: "An eye for an eye and a

tooth for a tooth" (Exodus 21:23-25; Leviticus 24:19-20).
Whatever happened to standing up for yourself?

Our language is colored with phrases that accept or
encourage retaliation: "She got what she deserved"; "He had
it coming to him"; "The bigger they are, the harder they fall."
Our government's penal code is built on paying for the crime
you've committed, and it is right to repay what can be repaid.
But Jesus is getting at something more than retribution. The
"but" that Jesus teaches here is a tough one. How does one
repay a punch in the face? What matches that? If the one who
punched me says, "I'm sorry, you can punch me back," that
might work. But if I, without being invited to do so, take it on
myself to punch the one who punched me, our run-in likely
would escalate into a full-blown fight, and my justification of
it would resemble a replay of my boyhood, playground
excuse: "He hit me first!" Such retaliation is based on my
assuming that I am right or that I am better than the one I am
punishing. I'm saying, "Don't mess with me!" I see myself as
the center of existence, as number one. In reality, I have put
myself in the place of God, who is the only real number one.
The apostle Paul picks up this teaching of Jesus and exhorts
us: "Dear friends, never take revenge. Leave that to the righteous anger of God. For the Scriptures say, 'I will take revenge;
I will pay them back,' says the Lord" (Romans 12:19 NLT).

The "but" Jesus requires here runs deep and goes against
the grain of our hearts and minds. He says we are not to
resist an evildoer, but are to turn the other cheek, offer our
cloak as well, go the second mile, and give to everyone who
asks. Is that what he means by going beyond the righteousness of the scribes and Pharisees? Possibly the only way we
can begin to understand what Jesus is teaching is to acknowledge that he knows what he is doing and wants us to learn
the kingdom way of life.

He did say he came "to fulfill the law," so that certainly
must be his purpose. Here, as in the other laws, he is present-

ing what the Godhead had planned from the beginning of time. He is teaching how *shalom* (peace, well-being) and *koinonia* (fellowship, community) can happen, and he is pointing to the reality of the peaceable kingdom and the re-creation of the garden of Eden. He is saying that kingdom life reflects the glory that is God's, that generous life is lived not for one's self but for others. In the kingdom of the heavens, membership is not about seeking greatness, but about humbly seeking the good of others. It's not about letting your anger boil over into murder or about men taking advantage of women in adultery and divorce. When everyone is honest, upright, and helpful, the kingdom blesses everyone around. And when everyone is satisfied with all things so generously shared, there is no need for selfishness. It is only because of selfishness that laws of retribution are needed. In a familiar passage of Scripture, the apostle Paul picks up this very matter:

> Do nothing out of selfish ambition or vain conceit. Rather, in humility value others above yourselves, not looking to your own interests but each of you to the interests of the others. In your relationships with one another, have the same attitude of mind Christ Jesus had: Who, being in very nature God, did not consider equality with God something to be used to his own advantage; rather he made himself nothing by taking the very nature of a servant, being made in human likeness. (Philippians 2:3-7 TNIV)

"Turn the other cheek" and "go the second mile" have become familiar phrases in the English language. Unfortunately, their use generally reflects a sense of awe that someone has done something extraordinary. They are not used to describe the normal situation. But Jesus is teaching that those actions are to be understood as normal for members of the kingdom of the heavens. Always turn the other cheek. Always go the second mile. And yes, if anyone sues you for your shirt, offer your coat, as well. If anyone asks for something, give what is needed.

A supreme example of kingdom generosity is found in Luke's Gospel as we hear of Zacchaeus, a chief tax collector in Jericho (see Luke 19:1-10). When Jesus invited himself to supper at Zacchaeus's house, Zacchaeus came into direct contact with the one who gave up his heavenly riches to become human, so that he might show human beings who God really is. In response, Zacchaeus became a new person in Christ; he received a spiritual heart transplant. To the people he had unlawfully wronged, he promised to restore not only the amount he had swindled but four times as much. To that Jesus declared, "Today salvation has come to this house" (Luke 19:9 NKJV).

By this time in Jesus' eye-opening explanation of God's law, we sense among the people pressing in around Jesus and within ourselves a vigorous mixture of response: wonder, disbelief, excitement, disagreement. But if we think Jesus has reached the climax of his interpretation with an examination of "an eye for an eye," we are bowled over by where he goes next. He plunges directly into his commentary on the sixth law, drawn from Leviticus 19:18: "You shall love your neighbor and hate your enemy" (verse 43). Beginning with the first law, "You shall not murder," Jesus has led us on a crescendo of revelation after revelation, gradually unfolding the rich and godly aim of living openly and generously with each other. But having reached this powerful juncture, he moves on even further to unveil the all-embracing and almost unbelievable principle of God's law: "But I say to you, Love your enemies and pray for those who persecute you" (verse 44).

In our uncertainness about arriving at such a spiritually elevated terrain, we find some comfort in the company we keep. We think of other Christians today and through the ages who have struggled with obeying such a demanding assignment. And we remember those loyal disciples who met Jesus at the mountain where he would ascend to heaven, and "they worshiped him; but some doubted" (Matthew 28:17). *The*

Message reports it this way: "Meanwhile, the eleven disciples were on their way to Galilee, headed for the mountain Jesus had set for their reunion. The moment they saw him they worshiped him. Some, though, held back, not sure about worship, about risking themselves totally" (verses 16-17).

Cautiously we ask if we couldn't be Jesus-followers just by obeying the written laws that have come down to us. Is it not enough to love just our neighbors? Why must we include enemies? Is that what total commitment requires? In Matthew 19 we find a young man caught in a similar predicament.

> Now behold, one came and said to Him, "Good Teacher, what good thing shall I do that I may have eternal life?" So He said to him, "Why do you call Me good? No one *is* good but One, *that is*, God. But if you want to enter into life, keep the commandments." He said to Him, "Which ones?" Jesus said, "'You shall not murder,' 'You shall not commit adultery,' 'You shall not steal,' 'You shall not bear false witness,' 'Honor your father and *your* mother,' and, 'You shall love your neighbor as yourself.'" The young man said to Him, "All these things I have kept from my youth. What do I still lack?" Jesus said to him, "If you want to be perfect, go, sell what you have and give to the poor, and you will have treasure in [the heavens]; and come, follow Me." But when the young man heard that saying, he went away sorrowful, for he had great possessions. (verses 16-22 NKJV)

The laws that we know and obey are not the source of rightness, but its course. Obedience to law does not create God's goodness but gives it freedom to flow. Even Jesus says he himself is not good—only God is good. The bad news, Jesus informs the wealthy landowner, is that his earthly possessions, according to God's generosity, do not belong to him alone, but to those in need. The good news is that, even after giving up his earthly possessions, he will have genuine treasure in the kingdom of the heavens. In God's economy, Jesus tells him, the blessings that come from God enrich not only those in need, but also those who distribute the blessings. In his announcement about the mutuality of God's kingdom, Jesus proclaimed, "Rejoice and be glad, for your reward is great in [the heavens]" (Matthew 5:12). It is in the kingdom of the heavens that we experience mutual generosity and joy, and abundant life in Christ. Nevertheless, we who meticulously keep the rules in order to be good, unmistakably find ourselves in alliance with the young man and silently retreat to ponder our situation. When we consider the responsibility of shouldering Jesus' incredible command to love our enemies, we ask, "Is it possible to live as Jesus commands?"

Nancy and I were talking with our friends Larry and Sue, an Episcopalian pastor and his wife, about the ups and downs of caring for aged parents. We agreed it was not always enjoyable but that we still desired to do it, even if a parent might not always be so lovable. Reflecting on the whole situation, Larry said, "There is no escape clause in 'Honor your father and mother' just as there is no escape clause in 'Love your enemies.'" He's right. Just because we don't relish caring for our parents during the tough times or don't comprehend how "Love your enemies" might work out for us in all situations, that does not invalidate God's word.

Religious scholar Karen Armstrong asks what many of us ask: "Does that mean that we are supposed to 'love' Hitler or Osama bin Laden?" Drawing on the thought of thirteenth-century theologian Thomas Aquinas, Armstrong suggests that love always seeks the good of others. We should know that "if we allow our rage and hatred to fester, this would not hurt our enemies—it would probably gratify them—but we ourselves would be diminished."[3]

We must caution ourselves at this point, however, not to take Jesus' instruction as another law. If I say, "To be a Christian I must love my enemies," I am making obedience to that law the source of goodness, instead of its result.

Through Jesus, God keeps telling us, "Be holy because I am holy" (Leviticus 19:2), "then you will love your enemies." Whether with the Beatitudes or other biblical commands, we always can fall easily into the pharisaical trap of obeying the rules as the ticket to rightness.

The *Martyrs Mirror* was first published by Anabaptists (rebaptizers) in Holland during the seventeenth century to encourage those who were being persecuted for living out their Christian faith. From that stately volume come the moving stories and testimonies of those who valued the righteousness of God's kingdom more than family or friends or home. No other story has so captivated the imagination of readers as the one about Dirk Willems, who in his late teens had been rebaptized upon his confession of faith in Jesus Christ. He had opened his house in Asperen, Holland, for others' baptisms and for the teaching of doctrines that the state church considered contrary to the Christian faith. For this he was hunted down and arrested.

> Concerning his apprehension, it is stated by trustworthy persons, that when he fled he was hotly pursued by a thief-catcher, and as there had been some frost, said Dirk Willems ran before over the ice, getting across with considerable peril. The thief-catcher following him broke through, when Dirk Willems, perceiving that the former was in danger of his life, quickly returned and aided him in getting out, and thus saved his life. The thief-catcher wanted to let him go, but the burgomaster very sternly called to him to consider his oath, and thus [Willems] was again seized by the thief-catcher.[4]

If he had run away, Willems could have gone free. But by living out the law of God's righteousness—by loving his enemies—he lived beyond the human law of self-preservation. For his resolute Christian faith, he was condemned to death by fire on May 16, 1569.

It is at this point in following Jesus' command to love our

enemies that the majority of Christians stop. We tend to say, "If Dirk Willems wants to love his enemies by giving up his life, that's his choice. But we can't do that as a nation. Our duty is to protect each other and our interests." But Jesus was speaking to all of his followers together: "Love your enemies." His instruction is for the kingdom of the heavens, for the church. So if it is for the church, how can the church go to war? We may say it is the country, not the church, that is going to war. But that's double-talk, and often it is the church and its leaders who encourage, even insist, that the country go to war. And is that to protect the kingdom of the heavens—or what? A popular bumper sticker states what is difficult for many Christians to say: "When Jesus said, 'Love your enemies,' I think he probably meant don't kill them."[5] On such a hot issue, how can the church find peace within itself in order to bring the gospel of reconciliation and peace to the world? It's hard enough to love our neighbors, how can we be expected to love our enemies? (Appendix 2: Positions on Peace offers further discussion.)

Jesus attaches a phrase to the sixth law that does not appear as a specific, written law anywhere else in the Bible: "and hate your enemy" (5:43). It is natural for us to hate enemies, and the psalmist speaks of hating God's enemies with "perfect hatred" (Psalm 139:22). For whatever reason, Jesus identifies such behavior as having gained the status of law in the eyes of his listeners. The reason the phrase is included here does not really matter, however, for it is what Jesus says immediately after it that rattles the rafters: "Love your enemies and pray for those who persecute you." Then in the same breath he adds, "so that you may be children of your Father in [the heavens]" (5:44-45). By this time in the Sermon, such a challenging and remarkable statement should come as no surprise. As we have seen throughout the discourse, this is the way God's righteousness comes. If we are children of the Father in the heavens, then the identifying characteristics of God will be seen in us. We will be the "spit-tin' image" of the Father.[6] So just as God makes the sun rise on the evil and on the good, and sends rain on the righteous and on the unrighteous, we also will value all people and show no bias toward one person over another. The Father in the heavens loves all people, whether they are enemies or not. "It's clear, isn't it," says Jesus, "that it's easy to love those who love you. Even scoundrels do that. And it's easy to give a pleasant greeting to those you know. Even godless pagans do that. But I am talking about God's goodness being mir-rored in the daily lives of the children of God. Just as your Father is the complete picture of righteousness, so should you be" (verses 46-48, PKC).

If there's one verse in the Bible that causes us to wince, it's "Be perfect, therefore, as your heavenly Father is perfect" (verse 48). To absorb the command to love our enemies is tough enough, but when we arrive at the point of needing to be perfect, we throw in the towel and give up on the whole Sermon. We conclude that if Jesus expects such an impossi-bility of us, then we know it's hopeless.

However, let me advocate for this verse. Jesus' directive is addressed to God's followers as a group, not to individuals in separation. Just as the whole Sermon—and the entire New Testament, for that matter—focuses on believers in commu-nity, so this verse speaks to the followers of Jesus together. The Greek is clear that as "children of your [plural] Father in the heavens" (verse 45), you (plural) are to be perfect "as your [plural] heavenly Father is perfect." Jesus is describing the character of the community that lives beyond the law in the presence of God's goodness.

Communities are made up of individuals, of course, but we westerners take this verse too individualistically and too much according to our current use of the word *perfect*. We think we are to live perfectly as individuals, with no flaws at all. Meanwhile, the character of the word *perfect* in the original text gets lost in translation; it requires numerous English words to capture its scope. *Perfect* in Greek (*telos*) imparts the concept of being complete, whole, finished, full grown, or fully developed. In 1 John 4:12 we find another use of the same word: "No one has ever seen God; if we love one another, God lives in us, and his love is perfected [*telos*] in us." The writer first states the obvious, "No one has ever seen God," but then reveals the almost unbelievable truth: "As we love each other, God comes among us, and God's love—righteousness and goodness—is perfected in us" (PKC). In the story from Matthew 19, we heard Jesus tell the wealthy young man, "If you want to be perfect [*telos*], go, sell . . . and give to the poor."

We cannot make God's love complete or fully developed in us as separated individuals, just as one person alone cannot sing a congregational hymn. In Matthew's fourth discourse, Jesus tells how communal love works: "Again I say to you that if two of you agree on earth concerning anything that they ask, it will be done for them by My Father in [the heavens]. For where two or three are gathered together in My name, I am there in the midst of them" (Matthew 18:19-20 NKJV).

For many years I thought those verses said that Jesus comes into our midst even when there are only two or three of us gathered in his name. And who would deny that Jesus does meet with just two or three, or even just one? But now I understand Jesus to be saying that decision-making in the church requires more than one person to be involved. One individual—pastor or layperson—cannot dictate the congregation's action just because "God told me!" Community is needed. Discernment in Christ's name by the community is always required for agreeing on earth "concerning anything they ask" so that the Father in the heavens might complete the action already desired in heaven. To be perfect, to be complete, means that everyone is counted as part of the whole. That is necessary for God's love to be perfected in the Christian community.

Jesus has been saying the same thing in the Sermon on the Mount. The kingdom of the heavens is a mutual community that carries out the righteousness of God by letting God's goodness come to life in everyday, human interaction. The blessings of that generous fellowship are available to all people and happen naturally, as the stream follows the watercourse. Members of that community do not claim greatness or aspire to it, but humbly seek the well-being of others. God alone is good, and God's holiness pervades those who are children of the Father.

Jesus has taken his hearers through six well-known laws to show that it is not only possible to go beyond their technicalities to fulfillment but also expected as a way of life. Those who pride themselves in blamelessly keeping the law are not any better than anyone else. In fact, they are in violation of the law by limiting its purpose and scope. By trying to hoard the blessings for themselves, they overlook the communal aspect of God's kingdom. They worship the letter of the law but do not internalize the spirit behind it. Jesus' concise and challenging mandate to "be perfect" rings in our ears as he brings this part of his sermon to a close. *The Message* puts it in our contemporary tongue: "In a word, what I'm saying is, Grow up. You're kingdom subjects. Now live like it. Live out your God-created identity. Live generously and graciously toward others, the way God lives toward you" (5:48).

For Discussion

Consider together the famous statement of evangelist Billy Sunday: "Going to church on Sunday will no more make you a Christian than parking a wheelbarrow in the garage will make it an automobile."

Don Shula, the longtime and highly respected professional football coach of the Baltimore Colts and Miami Dolphins, lost his temper at a referee's call. In that televised game he surprised millions of viewers when an open microphone caught his heated profanity. As letters of disapproval came pouring in from all over the country, Shula made no excuses but sent an apology to everyone who included a return address: "Thank you for taking time to write. Please accept my apologies for the remarks. I value your respect and will do my best to earn it again."[7] What can Shula's actions teach us?

Henry Wadsworth Longfellow wrote, "If we could read the secret history of our enemies, we should find in each man's life sorrow and suffering enough to disarm all hostility." What windows are flung open at that thought?

— 6 —

Minding the Mission
Why Even Pray?

When you are praying, do not heap up empty phrases as the Gentiles do; for they think that they will be heard because of their many words. Do not be like them, for your Father knows what you need before you ask him.

> Pray then in this way:
> Our Father in [the heavens],
> hallowed be your name.
> Your kingdom come.
> Your will be done,
> on earth as it is in heaven.
> Give us this day our daily bread.
> And forgive us our debts,
> as we also have forgiven our debtors.
> And do not bring us to the time of trial,
> but rescue us from the evil one.

For if you forgive others their trespasses, your heavenly Father will also forgive you; but if you do not forgive others, neither will your Father forgive your trespasses. (Matthew 6:7-15)

The Lord's Prayer is the keyhole through which we observe all the teaching of Jesus' Sermon, and it serves as the mission statement of God's kingdom. Matthew has placed it strategically at the Sermon's center, both physically and theologically.

After we look at it, we will come back and pick up the applications of Jesus' teaching beginning at 6:1.

Jesus leads into his kingdom prayer in 6:7-8, saying we should not babble like pagan peoples do, thinking that their many words can win favor with their gods. Putting it that way, I wonder if God will hear me because I pray long prayers or write out my prayers or pray extemporaneously. What if I recite certain formulas or use special words or lie flat on my face or raise my hands or fold my hands or close my eyes or kneel or stand? Jesus simply says, "Do not be like them." Then, immediately on the heels of that straightforward remark, he makes an astounding comment: "for your Father knows what you need before you ask him." If I think prayer is asking God to fulfill my personal desires, Jesus' comment is confusing. If our heavenly Father knows what we need even before we ask, why even pray?

Try this experiment. Hold one of your hands in front of you. Turn it over. Move it from side to side. Scratch your chin with your fingers. Now lay your hand in your lap. How did you get your hand and fingers and arm to complete those movements? It is clear that your thoughts controlled the action. You might say, "No, my muscles controlled them." But even then, how did your muscles control your hand? For each of us, the body is controlled by our thoughts and learned reflexes. But the body needs to be in working order to do that. All the nerves, muscles, ligaments, and bones need to be in tune with each other and the brain. In a sense, my body is my kingdom. If my hand rests on a hot stove, what happens? I quickly lift it off—that is, if my body is operating as designed. If my hand does not say to my brain, "Quick, pull me off!" my hand will stay on the hot stove and burn. Does my mind know what is good for my hand? Sure. All of us know that our hands will burn on a hot stove. But my hand must be in communication with my brain so that my body knows its hand is in terrible danger and will take it off.

Let's adjust the image. Suppose the physical body is God's kingdom, and the brain represents God the heavenly Father. Just as the human mind has functioning control over the body, so God has functioning control over the kingdom of God. God knows what is good for the kingdom. Jesus said, "Your Father knows what you need before you ask him" (*your* and *you* are both plural). But if a hand of God's kingdom is not in tune with other parts of the body and is not in communication with God-the-brain, how can the kingdom remove the hand from the hot stove? If the hand's prayers are concerned only with being strong and beautiful, the hand is neither in tune with other parts of the kingdom nor communicating appropriately with God. And its prayers fail.

The hand may be more concerned about fulfilling the law to pray than with staying in tune with God and others. It may be trying to impress other parts of the body and its brain that it is a good and loyal hand. It may even pray for miraculous displays such as sticking itself into a meat grinder to show others how God-the-brain will protect it from harm. But "do not be like them." Just as the self-serving pianist considers her showy technique to be the center of the performance rather than the means to the music, so our self-indulgent prayers get in the way of letting God's righteousness flow through us.

Prayer is a confession of faith in The One Who Is In Charge. Prayer is a pledge of allegiance to God's kingdom and its righteousness. If we count ourselves among God's kingdom people, the right way to pray is the way Jesus taught us.

Our Father in [the heavens], hallowed be your name. The Lord's Prayer is a community prayer. It is clear from the outset that it is *our* Father, not *my* Father. The account of the early church in Acts 2:42-47 reports that they had all things *in common*. It was a community of *ours*, not *mine*, and that is the image Jesus portrays in this model prayer and throughout his Sermon. Jesus uses the warm word *Father* to picture an attractive presence. Our Father to whom we pray is not distant from us or detached. The space and atmosphere directly around us comprise "the heavens," a place where the divine and human mingle. Contrary to the assumption that all gods are distant from their subjects and haughtily pursue their selfish pleasures, Jesus teaches us to pray to the loving Father who is close to us, who surrounds us, who is readily available to the community of the heavens.

Quite unbelievably, however, this Father who is close to us is at the same time The One Who Is Holy, untouchable, and set apart. The word translated as "hallowed be" reverently acknowledges God as the infinite and ageless I Am, the Yahweh of ancient times whose name is too holy to voice. When we utter, "Hallowed be your name," we reveal who God is. We are not just saying that God should be honored, nor do we have authority to make such an assertion. Just as in ancient times when the use of the name unveiled the essence of the one being named, so here the name of God is "Hallowed." God is holy, no matter what we say or do. All we can do is extol and confess the infinite presence who is beyond all human understanding. With awe, in chorus with the seraphim and cherubim and all the creatures surrounding the throne, we cry out, "Holy, holy, holy is the Lord God the Almighty" (Revelation 4:8).

Your kingdom come. Your will be done, on earth as it is in heaven. Echoing over land and sea, and riding "on the wings of the storm,"[1] comes God's almighty voice: "Be holy because I, the LORD your God, am holy" (Leviticus 19:2 TNIV). As human beings, we recoil from such direct encounter with God the Almighty. We "fear" the Lord, just as Moses took off his shoes and hid his face from seeing God when he came upon the burning bush (see Exodus 3:1-6); just as Isaiah responded with a lament on his own wretchedness when the pivots of the thresholds shook and the temple filled with smoke (see Isaiah 6:1-8); just as the children of Israel trembled at the loud blasting of the ram's horn as God's holiness engulfed the mountain in lightning and thunder and clouds (see Exodus 19:16-25).

But Jesus says, "Pray in this way . . . Your kingdom come. Your will be done, on earth as it is in heaven." Jesus says to pray to our Father in the heavens, who is also the holy and awesome God, that the kingdom of this holy-but-present God may come. Even more than that, we are to pray that God's kingdom come and that God's will be done *on earth*— now! We know it is now and not just some time in the future, because Jesus immediately instructs his hearers to pray for daily bread and to forgive each other, neither of which implies a future time when Jesus would rule unopposed. Jesus is giving instructions to common people on how to live God's righteousness from day to day—on earth.

Heaven is singular in the phrase "on earth as it is in heaven," contrary to the plural *heavens* of the previous verse. There *heavens* had indicated the closeness of the heavenly Father, but here the contrast of heaven and earth shows the great difference between heaven and earth. *Heaven* refers to somewhere distant from us, and *earth*, to our temporal habitat. Heaven is the place of God's holy throne, not earth's profaneness. Heaven is the place where Jesus came from, from which he emptied himself to take the form of a servant, becoming a human being on earth. In praying for the kingdom and will of God to show up on earth, we are praying that the miracle of God's holy presence become an earthly reality among us. When that happens, the kingdom of the heavens flourishes among us as both present and distant, a community where earth and heaven intersect in the present.

Sometimes we say, "That would be heaven on earth." In a real sense, that's what the kingdom of the heavens is—not that the whole *place* of heaven itself would move to earth from wherever it is, but that God's heavenly majesty, power, and righteousness would show up here. In addition, when Jesus teaches us to pray, "Your kingdom come," that is not a prayer for God's kingdom to come into existence. God's kingdom is already here, and Jesus makes it a possibility for our lives. Our prayer request is for God's existing kingdom to take over our lives. In the farewell address to his followers then and now, Jesus addresses that very idea (note that each *you* is plural):

> If you love me, keep my commands. And I will ask the Father, and he will give you another advocate to help you and be with you forever—the Spirit of truth. The world cannot accept him, because it neither sees him nor knows him. But you know him, for he lives with you and will be in you. (John 14:15-17 TNIV)

That is how God's kingdom comes! God's Spirit lives among us. If we choose to belong only to the kingdom(s) of this world, we cannot receive God's kingdom. If we as individuals and community selfishly rule our own little kingdoms, we do not see God or know the indwelling Spirit. When blinded by our inflated self-significance, we cannot ask that God's will be done. When self-righteously following our own perception of the letter of the law, we cannot be open to God's will being done among us.

"Your kingdom come, your will be done, on earth as it is in heaven" voices a petition and a cause that encompass the entire Sermon on the Mount. If we genuinely repent of self-sufficiency and control, God honors that prayer. It is only by divine grace that all the kingdoms of our lives can so unite with God's kingdom that all our individual kingdoms come together under divine will, and we live and reign together with God.

Give us this day our daily bread. We know bread. It is something we can relate to, something we can hold in our hands. Some of us bake our own bread and enjoy tasty varieties made from various grains and ingredients. Even so, I do not think of bread as "daily" bread. When Nancy and I were privileged to spend time in Europe, we discovered that people bought fresh bread every morning at the local bakeries. If we didn't buy some bread in the morning, we were out of luck later in the day. For me, that starts to describe "daily" bread. Add to that the constant daily struggle of those who are homeless and starving, and we begin to see not only the differences in national and ethnic customs, but also the absolute necessity of finding bread every day. To the people around Jesus, bread was a common and necessary food.

But besides its nutritional value, bread also carried a rich, religious meaning. To Jewish people it symbolized God's provision and care. The story of their deliverance from slavery in Egypt was repeated as if it had happened just yesterday. On their wilderness journey, even when they grumbled about not having food, God did not give up on them, but provided the miracle of manna. It appeared every morning like thin flakes of frost after the dew had gone. It became their *daily* bread, for if they collected more than enough for one day, it would rot. Their life was lived from day to day.

In the Lord's Prayer, most Bible versions say, "Give us this day our daily bread," while some substitute "today" for "this day." The emphasis is on what happens now, not yesterday or tomorrow, and certainly not on collecting more than is needed for a day. Phillips paraphrases it: "Give us this day the bread we need." When it's put that way, we see a broader scope than just physical bread, and the familiar words of Jesus come to mind: "I am the bread of life" (John 6:48). In a verse coming up soon in the Sermon, Jesus, the bread of life, touches on the need of daily sustenance: "Therefore do not worry about tomorrow, for tomorrow will worry about its own things. Sufficient for the day *is* its own trouble" (6:34 NKJV). Jesus gives us a clue that what we need is not just food to satisfy physical hunger, but nourishment to satisfy what we need for living. Whether it's the physical bread we need or the spiritual, our Father already knows what we need before we ask (6:8). So when we pray for daily bread, we are praying that our Father in the heavens may sustain our complete life while we commit ourselves to God's care in Jesus, the Bread of Life.

And forgive us our debts, as we also have forgiven our debtors. Debts, trespasses, sins. Is one right and the others wrong? No. It's a matter of tradition and choice.[2] All three words are found in and around the Lord's Prayer as it appears in Matthew and Luke. In a general sense, the differing words all indicate something lacking or owed. Matthew 6:12 literally says "debts" and "debtors." Luke 11:4 uses "sins" and "debtors." And immediately following the Lord's Prayer in Matthew, Jesus adds the third word: "For if you forgive others their trespasses, your heavenly Father will also forgive you; but if you do not forgive others, neither will your Father forgive your trespasses" (6:14-15). Whatever words we use, they do not alter the intent of the prayer. Offering forgiveness is a nonnegotiable condition for Jesus. Forgiveness, as part of its foundational role in the kingdom of the heavens, is one of the marvelous blessings that abound in the kingdom. Just as all blessings are gifts of God that become effective as they are passed on, so those who know true forgiveness themselves pass on forgiveness to others. When we don't forgive, it is a sign that we ourselves have not allowed God's forgiveness to give us a new heart.[3]

When high-profile public officials pull off their self-serving shenanigans, we say they should ask forgiveness or at least say they are sorry. But we cannot force others to ask forgiveness—we can only *give* them for*give*ness. In the same way, God cannot make us ask forgiveness but can only offer it. God's forgiveness is already established; it is up to us to accept it. "While we still were sinners Christ died for us" (Romans 5:8). God's forgiveness stands ready, but we are forgiven "as we also have forgiven our debtors." We must live out for others what God lived out for us in Christ. In forgiving others, it is we who find freedom. As Katie Funk Wiebe writes, "When we don't forgive [a person for an offense], we bind ourselves to that other person and destroy ourselves. Forgiveness releases us from bondage to that other person. We're free."[4]

Dan Snyder was a twenty-five-year-old who played for the Atlanta Thrashers of the National Hockey League. He died

October 5, 2003, of injuries suffered in Atlanta when a Ferrari driven by teammate Dany Heatley, twenty-two, went out of control at an estimated eighty miles per hours. Heatley was charged with a felony count of vehicular homicide. The entire Thrashers team and management, along with NHL Commissioner Gary Bettman and Toronto Maple Leafs players, attended the funeral service in Elmira, Ontario. As family members and the Atlanta players walked from the Snyder home to the church, dozens of young hockey players from Elmira and the surrounding area tapped their sticks on the street in tribute. "It was a sound every ounce as reverential as the lonely howl of a bugle," wrote *New York Times* columnist Selena Roberts.

What happened after the funeral service made the day extraordinary—not exceptional by kingdom of the heavens standards, but rare for what we normally experience. Graham Snyder, Dan's father, embraced the young Heatley and offered assurance of the family's forgiveness. Then he told everyone, "We are all human beings, and we know that humans make mistakes. We want you to know that we do not lay blame on Dany Heatley for the accident that took our son from us. . . . There is nothing to gain from harboring resentment or anger toward others. . . . Forgiveness is also part of being human." Roberts noted that the act of the Snyder family's choosing "the path of caring over condemnation . . . may save the rest of Heatley's life—emotionally, competitively and legally."[5]

But there is the other side of forgiveness too. As we saw earlier, Jesus teaches the Christian's duty of making things right if anyone holds something against us: "So if you are standing before the altar in the Temple, offering a sacrifice to God, and you suddenly remember that someone has something against you, leave your sacrifice there beside the altar. Go and be reconciled to that person. Then come and offer your sacrifice to God" (Matthew 5:23-24 NLT). When someone has offended me, I control the power to forgive or not to forgive. But on the other hand, if I have offended someone else, that person holds the power to forgive me or not. It is I who need to be forgiven. In order to be reconciled or to make restitution, I must relinquish any presumed control I claim and ask forgiveness. The offended one may not want to forgive me, and that is her choice. But I need to open myself to losing my pride about the good image I may think I've achieved, and admit that I've done wrong. It is tough to say, "I'm sorry. Would you forgive me?" But forgiveness is God's kingdom way, and reconciliation is the goal of forgiveness, whether we offer it or request it.

When any offense is committed between me and someone else, a break in relationship develops, and community is negatively affected. That involves the relationship between the two of us, between God and each of us, and between God and both of us together. Unavoidably, all unresolved offenses take a toll on the welfare of the whole community. Jesus says we should take care of any conflict in the community right away, so everyone can worship.

And do not bring us to the time of trial, but rescue us from the evil one. These words are quite different from those to which many have become accustomed: "And lead us not into temptation, but deliver us from evil" (6:13 KJV). Starting at the end of the verse, we note that numerous Bible versions use "the evil one" instead of "evil." It is a matter of choice, since the Greek can be translated either way. Both interpretations mean essentially the same thing, *evil* being a reference to evil in general and "the evil one" referring to the devil. *Rescue* and *deliver* are two words that mean the same thing. When we sing the spiritual, "Didn't my Lord deliver Daniel," it is clear that Daniel was rescued. All through the stories of the Bible when God's people cry out to be delivered from the evil one, and God remembers them, we know that a divine "rescue operation is about to be staged."[6]

Should we say "lead us not into temptation" or "do not

bring us to the time of trial"? Both *temptation* and *trial* are valid translations. William Barclay, renowned Scottish theologian of the last century, deals with that question in his book on the Lord's Prayer. He concludes that the Greek word for temptation contains three ideas that are relevant for use here. First, testing or evaluating the quality of a person or thing, such as checking to see if a cake is done. Second, putting a person in a situation that is really a test, but involves the possibility of failure, such as seeing if you can run a four-minute mile. Third, a deliberate invitation and seduction to sin, such as my inviting you to help me rob a bank. Barclay says the difficulty here is that no one English word can do justice to these various ideas.[7] So we must say that temptations and trials come in many sizes and shapes, and we need help with all of them.

Even so, what does Jesus mean? Should we expect to have all trials removed from us? And besides that, if we did not ask otherwise, would our Father in the heavens really lead us into temptation? According to Barclay, the Hebrew mind, knowing that all things are in the hands of God, would not have had the difficulty with this phrase that we do. Even temptation somehow fits into God's purpose and plan. It is part of our human situation, just as it was part of what Jesus experienced in coming to this world. So we need help.

Certainly we come to God asking that we not face more than we can bear of trials that are sure to come. The petition itself might be very much like an athlete asking the beloved trainer, "Go easy with me! Don't push me too hard!" Barclay concludes (and I like how he contrasts theologians and human beings), "For the theologian the theological problem may be there; for the human being the theological problem is lost in the instinctive appeal of the human need."[8]

But another issue lingers for me. The Lord's Prayer is a kingdom prayer, a community prayer to *our* Father in the heavens. We do not pray, "And do not bring *me* to the time of trial, but rescue *me* from the evil one." I can so easily slip into praying for myself, since I see the world through my own eyes instead of from the kingdom's perspective. What does it mean to pray for *us* not to be brought to trial, but for *us* to be rescued from the evil one? The petition immediately follows our request to be forgiven as we forgive, a foundational principle of the kingdom. Might we as a community be tempted to retain individual power by not forgiving each other? Might we refuse to forgive others because we want to see them suffer while they pay for what they've done? The mutual, generous kingdom of the heavens can exist, but only by nurturing the freedom that forgiveness allows.

More generally, the kingdom fellowship might pray for deliverance from abusing the various characteristics Jesus has addressed so far in the Sermon: blessings are for all people, not just for us; the kingdom is one of mutuality, not oppressive hierarchy; following the letter of the law is to be surpassed by living beyond the law, whether dealing with murder, adultery, divorce, oaths, retaliation, or prejudice. As Jesus continues in the Sermon, he will teach about the righteousness of the kingdom in its spiritual, material, and social dimensions. All of these are areas of potential temptation from which the Christian community needs to be rescued.

In a dramatic way, our deliverance by God from the evil one is illustrated by the story Jesus tells at the end of the Sermon (7:24-27). Those who are wise build on the rock; those who are foolish build on the sand. And their work is tested by the wind and the rain and the floods. I like to think that his parable shows how to prevent trouble before it happens, a kind of *preventive* rescue. Usually I think of rescue or deliverance as happening after we get into trouble. But why wait? Let those who have ears, listen! If we hear the words of Jesus and put them into practice, our community will stand because it is built on rock. If we build on the sand of our selfish power and wisdom, look out! There will be a great fall.

For thine is the kingdom, and the power, and the glory, for ever. Amen (6:13 KJV). Although this magnificent doxology is regularly repeated by worshippers in the western church, it does not show up in many Bible translations. In Protestant worship it is included in audible prayer. In Catholic worship (the Mass), the community prays the Lord's Prayer as part of the communion rite, but without adding the doxology. Then the presider prays, "Deliver us, Lord, from every evil, and grant us peace in our day. In your mercy keep us free from sin and protect us from all anxiety as we wait in joyful hope for the coming of our Savior, Jesus Christ." Then the entire community prays, "For the kingdom, the power and the glory are yours, now and forever. Amen." As a very young man, I remember looking up the Lord's Prayer in the Bible and being struck not only by the inconsistencies between the biblical words and those I knew but also by the different words in Matthew and Luke. But as long as we need to translate the Bible from the original biblical languages, we're going to come up with differing versions.

Another consideration is that of original text. It is the agreement among many Bible scholars that the best existing manuscripts of the Bible do not include "For thine is the kingdom, and the power, and the glory, for ever. Amen." It is customary in Jewish tradition to say a doxology to end a prayer, and one common way of doing that is to add it as a private prayer. So although a doxology is expected after the Lord's Prayer, it need not appear in the written text.[9] But the marvelous doxology that has come down to us does appear in some of the later manuscript fragments of the Bible and has been described as "a scribal alteration for liturgical purposes based on 1 Chronicles 29:11-13."[10] If so, that doxology obviously became a cherished worship response to the Lord's Prayer and was written down by a copyist, later becoming part of a particular manuscript.

In the world of classical music we find a similar practice

when a cadenza is inserted during the performance of a concerto for solo instrument and orchestra. The orchestra stops playing and the soloist sounds alone, recalling and embellishing themes from the concerto, very much like a jazz musician improvising a solo while the rest of the ensemble sits out. A cadenza is sometimes improvised as well and in its way becomes a kind of doxology. It may be prepared and written out by the performer or created by the composer, and can take on the status of a standard "response" for that particular concerto.

The majestic and moving text of King David's prayer in 1 Chronicles 29:11-13 easily could have shaped the doxology of the Lord's Prayer.

> Thine, O LORD, *is* the greatness, and the power, and the glory, and the victory, and the majesty: for all *that is* in the heaven and in the earth *is thine*; thine *is* the kingdom, O LORD, and thou art exalted as head above all. Both riches and honour *come* of thee, and thou reignest over all; and in thine hand *is* power and might; and in thine hand *it is* to make great, and to give strength unto all. Now therefore, our God, we thank thee, and praise thy glorious name. (1 Chronicles 29:11-13 KJV)

Those are kingdom words—God's kingdom! To think that worshippers in the earliest centuries after Christ may have taken those words to create a doxology for the Lord's Prayer is an exhilarating thought. It gives me goose bumps. By ardently voicing such a doxology, we are not heaping up empty phrases as the godless peoples do, but are praying the kingdom prayer, committing ourselves to God's rule of righteousness.

Surely there is no better way to close the Lord's Prayer than to join hands with the church throughout the centuries, standing up to joyfully and energetically cry out, "For thine is the kingdom, and the power, and the glory, forever. Amen!"

How could we better summarize and conclude and celebrate our pledge of allegiance to God's kingdom?

Can you imagine raising the roof every Sunday morning with that hosanna? I wonder how often we as twenty-first-century Christians merely repeat those words as if we're reading nutrition facts off a cereal box. Whether the doxology consists of Christ's words or was added by faithful Christians, it enthusiastically and festively proclaims the teaching of Jesus in his model prayer. The Lord's Prayer is not about us—it's about God. It's not about human desires and resources—it's about the power and glory and kingdom of God. Oh, yes, we're involved, but we're not in control. It is God's kingdom and God's power and God's glory—forever! Amen.

For Discussion

Wendell Berry's fictional character Jayber Crow reflects, "Does prayer change God's mind? If God's mind can be changed by the wants and wishes of us mere humans, as if deferring to our better judgment, what is the point of praying to Him at all? And what are we to think when two good people pray for opposite things—as when two devout mothers of soldiers on opposite sides pray for the safety of their sons, or for victory?"[11] What guidance do we receive from the kingdom prayer of our Lord?

Could the Lord's Prayer serve as a mission statement for your small group or congregation?

Sometimes Luke 4:18-19 is looked on as the mission statement of Jesus. How does that strike you?

Spiritual Secrets
When Rewards Are Not Awards

Beware of practicing your piety before others in order to be seen by them; for then you have no reward from your Father in [the heavens].

So whenever you give alms, do not sound a trumpet before you, as the hypocrites do in the synagogues and in the streets, so that they may be praised by others. Truly I tell you, they have received their reward. But when you give alms, do not let your left hand know what your right hand is doing, so that your alms may be done in secret; and your Father who sees in secret will reward you.

And whenever you pray, do not be like the hypocrites; for they love to stand and pray in the synagogues and at the street corners, so that they may be seen by others. Truly I tell you, they have received their reward. But whenever you pray, go into your room and shut the door and pray to your Father who is in secret; and your Father who sees in secret will reward you. . . .

And whenever you fast, do not look dismal, like the hypocrites, for they disfigure their faces so as to show others that they are fasting. Truly I tell you, they have received their reward. But when you fast, put oil on your head and wash your face, so that your fasting may be seen not by others but by your Father who is in secret; and your Father who sees in secret will reward you. (Matthew 6:1-6, 16-18)

One day, at a church-related retreat center, I talked with a woman who worked there, and it was obvious she was feeling overwhelmed. She was a bit harried and complained with dour face and downturned corners of the mouth, "It's hard work, and it's low pay, but it's my mission." I didn't know whether to laugh or cry. Although she had given herself to the Lord's work, the joy of serving Christ was not visible. I commend her for serving Christ in that mission, and I do not believe she was doing it to impress others. But I could not imagine that her situation was an accurate or favorable picture of God's kingdom appearing among us and God's will being done on earth as it is in heaven.

During his forty days and nights in the wilderness (see Matthew 4:1-11) and throughout his ministry, Jesus was tempted to abandon his mission of righteousness and win a popular following. But to do so would mean giving up the righteousness that formed the very core of his life and mission. He could turn stones into bread to provide miraculous surpluses of everyday needs, but that would be abusing his economic (material) trust. He could throw himself off the pinnacle of the temple to make institutionalized religion rally around him, but that would turn his religious (spiritual) leadership into flashy showmanship. He could gain control of all the political (social) kingdoms of the world he surveyed from the mountaintop, but that would be misusing his heavenly powers in earthly ways. But Jesus passed the test! He did not give in to turning God's generous righteousness into an oppressive system of arrogant and selfish control.

Knowing that kind of temptation, Jesus passionately taught his followers how to remain faithful and verify God's goodness in their lives. In the Sermon on the Mount, he conveys to the crowds, to the disciples, and to us the servant posture of the spiritual, material, and social dimensions of righteousness. The spiritual dimensions deal with relationship to God (6:1-6, 16-18), the material dimensions with relationship to physical surroundings (6:19-34), and the social dimensions with relationship to other people (7:1-12). Jesus was concerned that the community be complete in God's will and purpose—"perfect"—in order to embody the servant life that he himself so graciously accepted and demonstrated. The blessings of God's kingdom, he said, are to be lived now. They are not reserved for some future time in heaven, but are down-to-earth gifts of grace that appear in the common, everyday, practical life of the Christian community.

In Matthew 6:1-18, interrupted purposely by the Lord's Prayer (verses 7-15), Jesus uses alms, prayer, and fasting to illustrate the spiritual dimensions of God's righteousness. Those three acts of devout worship differ from each other only in the activity involved, since each example is a picture of how Christian disciples relate their lives to God's will. Jesus' emphasis is not on proper technique for doing righteous acts but on being centered on the presence of the Father, who is always present in secret. The "doing" naturally follows the "being." The Lord's Prayer itself models that approach, starting with seeking the presence of the Father in the heavens and "hallowing" his name. To emphasize that focus at the outset of this segment (6:1), Jesus summarizes what he is teaching in the three examples and establishes the ground rules: What you do is not for you, but for your Father in the heavens.

As we know, Jesus wants his followers to live by the intent of the law, not by its rigid technicalities. God's righteousness comes as we live beyond the rules of law and as we put into practice the attitude and purpose that lie beyond the law. If we truly live in God's righteousness by locating ourselves within the source of goodness, we fulfill the rules without being self-conscious about it. In 6:1 Jesus reminds his listeners, literally, "not to do your righteousness" before others (PKC). The arrogance of those who want to be great in the kingdom by doing their righteous acts for public approval is glaringly apparent to the Father in the heavens. Meanwhile, the humble service of those who live in faithful devotion to God and for the welfare of others, as Christ did, is just as apparent to the Father, and those acts are rewarded.

Aren't we glad that we have company in relating to Jesus, that Jesus chose disciples who were so much like us? If Jesus had chosen flawless religious specimens to follow him, we wouldn't quite know how to proceed. In *Gifts: The Joy of Serving God*, authors John Ortberg, Laurie Pederson, and Judson Poling write,

> Jesus knew that his own followers would wrestle with the Messiah complex, so he decided to put them in a small group together. And sure enough, one day they "argued about who was the greatest" (Mark 9:34). Hang out with a group of people long enough, and the Messiah complex will rear its ugly head.
>
> So Jesus took a little child, and . . . in effect said, "Here's your ministry. Give yourselves to those who can bring you no status or clout. You need to help this child not just for her sake but more for your sake. For if you don't, your whole life will be thrown away on an idiotic contest to see who is the greatest. But if you serve her—often and well and cheerfully and out of the limelight—then the day may come when you do it without thinking, 'What a wonderful thing I've done.' Then you will begin serving naturally, effortlessly, for the joy of it. Then you will begin to understand how life in the kingdom works.[1]

We will see, when we come to the close of the Sermon, that Jesus turns away all those who expect to enter the kingdom of the heavens on the basis of what they consider their great deeds (see 7:22-23). That kind of situation is reported again in the final discourse of Matthew, where those who think of their own deeds as being righteous are sent to eternal punishment, but those who have humbly embodied the righteousness of God are sent to eternal life (see 25:46). In his Sermon, when Jesus announced the mutuality of the kingdom of the heavens, he challenged everyone to let the light of God's righteousness shine in their community, so others might see their good works and bring glory to God (see 5:16). Those good works do not originate in people's own minds and hearts as acts of greatness but come from God's righteousness, which is by nature humble and seeks the salvation of all people.

When a former high-school student started an annual scholarship in Cheryl O'Connor's name, she was honored and humbled. "I know there are thousands of teachers who impact students' lives," she said. "I was just fortunate to run into one that wanted to give back." Melvin Glover, a 1994 graduate of Lima (Ohio) Senior High School and now a medical doctor in Savannah, Georgia, came from a family that did not have money for college, so scholarships were critical for him. He said O'Connor, his guidance counselor, would personally put applications in his hand. "She meant so much to me. I wanted to start it in her honor," he said. "She made sure I explored every educational and financial option out there." The Glover-O'Connor Scholarship of one thousand dollars is given each year to both a male and female student, and Glover would like to eventually increase the amount.[2]

O'Connor was not working for a reward; she was faithfully doing her job of guiding a student. But her action was rewarded. Jesus, as he begins his teaching on the spiritual dimensions of righteousness, brings back the term *reward*: "Be careful not to do your 'acts of righteousness' in front of others, to be seen by them. If you do, you will have no reward from your Father in [the heavens]" (6:1 TNIV). In connection with 5:11-12 ("your reward is great in the heavens") we briefly discussed the idea of reward. But now it is important to take a further look, because reward is a dominant factor in the examples of alms, prayer, and fasting.

Two continuing habits contribute to making our understanding a bit foggy. First, we tend to regard rewards variously as prizes for what we have accomplished, for being the best, or for doing something we see as extraordinary. That is not how Jesus spoke of them in his Sermon, as we discussed earlier. Second, when the Greek word for "heavens" is not translated in the plural, and we read "your Father in heaven," we tend to think that rewards are handed out only on "the Last Day" in heaven, in that faraway place, distant in time and space. But this verse is speaking about our Father in the heavens—here, now, around us. Our misperceptions add up to believing that because we do great works for the kingdom, we will be awarded jewels in our crowns when we finally get to heaven (and the more jewels we have, the better we'll look). In addition, we think that all the sacrifices we make here on earth for Christ will have been worth it when we finally get those jewels. Is that the nature of the spiritual dimensions of righteousness? What does it mean for us not to display our righteousness before others so that we do not miss the reward of our Father in the heavens?

Let's answer those questions as we move into the three examples of alms, prayer, and fasting. All three are clearly marked by their opening and closing words, beginning with "When you" and ending with "your Father who sees in secret will reward you." Reward is mentioned twice in each example, first in relation to hypocrites who seek recognition for publicly doing what they think of as righteous deeds, and second in relation to Christ's disciples as they follow his teaching of humility and faithfulness. Two different Greek words are used for the two instances in each scene, but both are often translated with only the one English word *reward*. Such a rendering is accurate as far as being literal, but subtle meanings are lost. The first instance of *reward* in each scene uses the same word that appeared in 6:1 for *reward* and has a meaning related directly to doing God's will. According to the *Theological Dictionary of the New Testament*,

> The distinctiveness of the divine reward is so radical . . . that if a man seeks human recognition and earthly

gain for his acts he thereby forfeits the acceptance which God wills to grant him in the [reward]. . . . For God's rewarding generosity is only for pure obedience which is free from all selfish calculation or external display.[3]

The second instance of reward in each scene employs a Greek word that picks up on the idea of being repaid, an interpretation found in a few familiar Bible versions. It can be seen as a kind of return on one's investment. Here the Father who sees in secret fulfills the divine obligation to bless the truly righteous acts of those who give alms, pray, and fast in secret, none of it done for arrogant display. They are rewarded as a matter of course, because that is the way God works, and not because the doing of the acts is a great accomplishment.

Consider the farmer who fertilizes, plows, plants, and cultivates so that the awaited crop can grow. The resulting harvest is not a prize for having done the work so well or for having decided to do it. Rather, it is a reward, a payback, for fulfilling the necessary actions that allow the crop to grow according to God's all-powerful plan. To be sure, doing the work well can increase the harvest. And that is what Jesus is talking about here: Do your spiritual acts of righteousness as God intends, and you'll reap a harvest of God's blessings. Such a pattern is evident in the brief, marvelous verse of James 3:18: "Peacemakers who sow in peace reap a harvest of righteousness" (TNIV).

A missionary related the following story told by two pastors of the church involved. Names, places, and certain words have been changed for reasons of safety and sensitivity, but the story, used here by permission, is true and its details are accurate.

In 1997 a prophetic word was given to the leaders of the Kingdom Church. The word was this: There will be an economic collapse, the president will be ousted, then an interim president, a woman president, then revival. After receiving this word they went to prayer and believed that they needed to respond to the first part of the word.

If there was going to be an economic collapse, what should they do? They believed they were told to pay all the bills of the church for a year. They did that with the funds they had on account. They then had remaining funds and asked, What do we do with the extra money we have? They went to prayer and the Lord told them to love their neighbor. The question was asked, Do you mean the actual neighbors around the church? They believed that is exactly what he was saying.

They set up food programs to feed five thousand poor non-Christian families in the slums around their church. They also did programs with the children and taught the illiterate how to read. They wanted to raise the opportunities to improve the lives of these "neighbors."

During the riots of 1998, a mob came to burn down the church building. There were about thirty staff inside the building at the time. The local non-Christians formed a human chain around the church and told the mob, "You can burn any church in this city, but you are not going to burn this one."

In the next six months the church grew from four thousand to seven thousand. I have wondered what the "neighbors" were defending when they stood down the mob. I believe they liked having "Jesus as their neighbor"—because this church was operating like Jesus.

Because the Kingdom Church showed the Lord's concern and love for the lost, the Lord blessed that ministry. The church is now about fifteen thousand in size.

Who could have predicted such a response from the local non-Christian people? The Father who sees in secret was rewarding the Kingdom Church for their beautiful and generous alms.

The spiritual dimensions of righteousness are reflected in the Lord's Prayer: "Your kingdom come. Your will be done, on earth as it is in heaven." To offer oneself as an earthly instrument of divine will is what God blesses and is clearly reflected in the humble act of almsgiving, even if (especially if) no one else notices. If I give alms to impress others, that's the only reward I get. But if I give out of God's love for the purpose of helping the poor, whether someone else notices or not, God rewards that action. And the amount one gives is not mentioned. God's reward is based on the way it is given and the purpose for which it is given. That reminds me of the story narrated in Mark's Gospel, a temple scene that teaches so dramatically the same godly truth:

> Jesus also taught: "Beware of these teachers of religious law! For they like to parade around in flowing robes and receive respectful greetings as they walk in the marketplaces. And how they love the seats of honor in the synagogues and the head table at banquets. Yet they shamelessly cheat widows out of their property and then pretend to be pious by making long prayers in public. Because of this, they will be more severely punished." Jesus sat down near the collection box in the Temple and watched as the crowds dropped in their money. Many rich people put in large amounts. Then a poor widow came and dropped in two small coins. Jesus called his disciples to him and said, "I tell you the truth, this poor widow has given more than all the others who are making contributions. For they gave a tiny part of their surplus, but she, poor as she is, has given everything she had to live on." (Mark 12:38-44 NLT)

From that story, Jesus' mention of "long prayers in public" by the shameless religious leaders brings us directly to the second dimension of kingdom spirituality: prayer. Here again the hypocrites get what they pray for: recognition by the people around them. Unhappily for them, however, even though they get their thrills from public recognition, they end up cheating not only the widows but themselves, as well. By centering their righteousness on what they themselves do, they unknowingly bypass God's reward, God's blessing. They are "praying" for their own little kingdoms, not for God's will to be done or for God's kingdom to show up on earth. Their view of God's kingdom is to keep everything tightly under their control.

Genuine prayer is not a performance to impress others—people or God. I may tell others that I pray often or that I spend a lot of time in devotions or that I do devotions in an exceedingly holy way or that God speaks to me because I am especially spiritual. But then Jesus says, "You've already got your reward. You won't get a response from God." That kind of spirituality is focused on myself, not on God, and God's kingdom is harmed by such action and attitude. As Jesus' teaching shows, church leaders can cleverly divert attention away from their self-serving acts by publicly making a show of how caring and "religious" they are. As the familiar adage says, "When your point is weak, pound the pulpit."

Praying for my own needs—to do well on a test, to win a ball game, to be safe on the highway, to get a raise in salary—can be self-serving and, therefore, damaging to the community. Is it that I want to control everything, especially my own life? We cry out to God when we get into trouble, and we contact everyone we can think of to pray for our specific needs. But when we are not experiencing trouble or are not desiring that something special happen in our lives, what is our desire? What is it we pray for then? Do we pray at all?

And is it as individuals that we pray, or do we pray as members of the community of Christ? The Lord's Prayer is offered from the community: "*Our* Father in the heavens, your kingdom come." If we actually are in community, by definition the community already is aware of our individual needs, and our corporate prayer rises as a community petition. Members of active communities know each other's joys

and sorrows, needs and commitments. Certainly it is important to pray for personal needs, but that is not the focus of
the community. If we pray for God's kingdom to come on
earth as it is in heaven, our personal needs find their answers
in the righteousness of that kingdom.

The third example of spiritual righteousness, the act of
fasting, offers the same recurring lesson: commitment to
righteousness is not for public display but for genuine devotion to God. With fasting, I am tempted to show others how
tough it is to do what I'm doing and how great a sacrifice I
am making for the cause of Christ. ("See how committed I
am!") Jesus says, "Don't try to show off your Christianity by
what you do for me. Instead of looking dismal to attract sym-
pathy, shampoo your hair and wash your face, and look the
best that you can look. Let everyone see that your life is totally together. My kingdom life is full of joy!" (PKC).

The apostle Paul knew that the Christians in Philippi
were quite human, but he also knew how divine power could
work in them and through them to bring God joy: "Do all
things without murmuring and arguing, so that you may be
blameless and innocent, children of God without blemish in
the midst of a crooked and perverse generation, in which you
shine like stars in the world" (Philippians 2:14-15). That is
not a law the apostle is giving them. He's giving them encouragement to live out God's righteousness right where they are.
Sure, they are human, but as God's people they also shine like
stars in the cosmos.

The first order of business for the church is to be church, to
carry out the message of God's reconciliation in their everyday
setting. The epistle of 1 Peter calls the church "a chosen race, a
royal priesthood, a holy nation, God's own people" in order to
proclaim the marvelous mercy it has received from God (2:9-
11). Then Peter says, "Live such good lives among the pagans
that, though they accuse you of doing wrong, they may see your
good deeds and glorify God on the day he visits us" (verse 12

TNIV). We heard that challenge from Jesus in the Sermon on the Mount: "In the same way, let your light shine before others, that they may see your good deeds and glorify your Father in [the heavens]" (Matthew 5:16 TNIV). That's a law that is not a law. That's the law of God's righteousness. It is our rule of faith. It is doing the will of the Father in the heavens.

With the examples of alms, prayer, and fasting, Jesus has outlined the spiritual dimensions of God's righteousness. Righteousness on earth is about the kingdom and the will of our Father in the heavens. However, as Christians we have become obsessed with our individual performance (obeying the rules) and personal sanctification (level of holiness), as if we might create the perfect example of what it means to be Christian. And that becomes our witness to "the world": "We can do it! So can you!" If that is our narrow view of God's kingdom and the sum of our Christianity, we as individuals and churches come off as entirely arrogant. As a result, we give the impression that we see ourselves as exemplary Christians, donating large financial gifts, offering prestigious prayers, and enduring great sacrifices, all in the name of being good. As a result, the church appears to be an exclusive club, spending God's money on selfish interests, claiming to know the true way, and looking down a self-righteous, judgmental nose at appalling sin in the surrounding community.

But, we ask, if we as the church are not to show off how well we obey God's laws, are not to tell others that our Christian life is better than their non-Christian life, and are not to speak out in judgment of the sin around us, what is our evangelistic message to be? John Fischer invites the church to confess,

> *We are not as good as we make ourselves out to be, but we aren't exactly getting that point across to the world.* Well, believe it or not, this is the point we need to be making. Our sins and doubts and mistakes are no threat to our witness: they are an integral part of

it. In its simplest form, our greatest witness to the world is to show and tell how much we need Jesus. Yes, the pronoun is right. Though our job may seem to have been to show people how much *they* need Jesus, we now as recovering Pharisees have a new job description: to show people how much *we* need Jesus. [4]

Jesus teaches that God's kingdom comes to earth in the humble life of devotion and service that does not seek recognition but in all honesty "tells it like it is." It is Christ's life and teaching and salvation we are proclaiming, not ours. The first chapter of Rick Warren's popular book *The Purpose-Driven Life* begins with the words "It's not about you."[5] It's about God's kingdom, God's purpose, God's will. But we tend to make ourselves the center of everything. Henry Blackaby says we should put our life commitment to God in perspective: "'What is God's will for my life?' is not the best question to ask. I think the right question is simply, 'What is God's will?' Once I know God's will, then I can adjust my life to Him and His purposes."[6]

When we put ourselves at the disposal of the awesome God we serve, God carries out the divine purpose through us in whatever way is appropriate, and that's what we want. It is not about whether we get the credit for doing it or that we've done it right while others are doing it wrong.

When James speaks of the power of prayer, he includes more than the healing of the sick.

> And the prayer offered in faith will make them well; the Lord will raise them up. If they have sinned, they will be forgiven. Therefore confess your sins to each other and pray for each other so that you may be healed. The prayer of a righteous person is powerful and effective. (5:15-16 TNIV)

What a marvelous gift of grace! These words reflect the same focus as the mission statement of the Lord's Prayer, which sits right in the middle of Jesus' examples of alms, prayer, and fasting. Could I—could the church—confess to the sin of self-righteousness? Could the countless fellowships of Christ's people in neighborhoods around the world confess our sin to each other and pray in the manner of James 5:16—that we may be forgiven so we may be healed? What a wonderful way to pray for God's kingdom to come and for God's will to be done on earth as it is in heaven!

God be merciful to us, sinners that we are, and grant us peace. Amen.

For Discussion

Is it ever appropriate to tell others what you've donated to charity or done for others?

To fast means to refrain from something for a specific purpose. For instance, certain blood tests require that we fast from food for twelve hours prior to being tested. To nurture our spiritual lives, it can be helpful to fast from certain foods or activities. Create a list for fasting that might be helpful to you: whole days without eating, or possibly items of food such as chocolates, meats, pastries, coffee, soft drinks, alcohol. What about TV watching, sports activities, hobbies? How can "prayer and fasting" nurture spirituality?

In Luke 18:9-14 Jesus is speaking to people who think of themselves as righteous but despise others. He compares two people who went to the temple to pray. The tax collector was justified (made righteous) by his prayer, but the Pharisee was not. Why? Put the story into the language of today.

— 8 —

Material Matters
You Get as You Give

Do not store up for yourselves treasures on earth, where moth and rust consume and where thieves break in and steal; but store up for yourselves treasures in heaven, where neither moth nor rust consumes and where thieves do not break in and steal. For where your treasure is, there your heart will be also.

The eye is the lamp of the body. So, if your eye is healthy, your whole body will be full of light; but if your eye is unhealthy, your whole body will be full of darkness. If then the light in you is darkness, how great is the darkness!

No one can serve two masters; for a slave will either hate the one and love the other, or be devoted to the one and despise the other. You cannot serve God and wealth.

Therefore I tell you, do not worry about your life, what you will eat or what you will drink, or about your body, what you will wear. Is not life more than food, and the body more than clothing? Look at the birds of the air; they neither sow nor reap nor gather into barns, and yet your heavenly Father feeds them. Are you not of more value than they? And can any of you by worrying add a single hour to your span of life? And why do you worry about clothing? Consider the lilies of the field, how they grow; they neither toil nor spin, yet I tell you, even Solomon in all his glory

127

was not clothed like one of these. But if God so clothes the grass of the field, which is alive today and tomorrow is thrown into the oven, will he not much more clothe you—you of little faith? Therefore do not worry, saying, "What will we eat?" or "What will we drink?" or "What will we wear?" For it is the Gentiles who strive for all these things; and indeed your heavenly Father knows that you need all these things. But strive first for the kingdom of God and his righteousness, and all these things will be given to you as well.

So do not worry about tomorrow, for tomorrow will bring worries of its own. Today's trouble is enough for today. (Matthew 6:19-34)

Millard Fuller, founder and president of Habitat for Humanity International, asks, "How radical is it to ask Christians to live out Jesus' Sermon on the Mount? What does it mean to truly love your neighbors and even your enemies as you love yourself?"[1] Fuller says that no one took the teaching of Jesus more seriously than Clarence Jordan, founder of Koinonia Farm in Americus, Georgia. In his foreword to Ann Louise Coble's book on Jordan and the Koinonia Farm, he describes how Jordan's "experiment" in pacifism, racial equality, and community living changed his life. Fuller and his wife, Linda, had been living in affluence in Montgomery, Alabama, when they arrived at Koinonia for a couple of hours but stayed a month. Fuller was at a critical juncture in his life, and although he had been raised in church, he had never met the Jesus Jordan followed so faithfully. Jordan constantly reminded him "that Jesus called on us to love our neighbors as we love ourselves."

When the Fullers returned to Koinonia in mid-1968, Millard worked with Jordan daily. One of their regular discussions was on providing housing for low-income neighbors, and as a result they launched a program called Partnership Housing. But Jordan's sudden death in October 1969 came before even one house could be finished. Out of faithful commitment, the Fullers along with others kept developing that program in south Georgia.

After a few years, the Fuller family went to Africa, where they began a similar program, patterned on the work they had done at Koinonia. When they returned to the states in 1976, they met "in an old abandoned chicken barn at Koinonia" and organized Habitat for Humanity to address issues of housing. From that modest beginning, Habitat has built more than 200,000 houses around the world and has provided more than a million people in more than three thousand communities with safe, decent, affordable shelter. With no end in sight!

In Matthew 6:19-34 Jesus shifts from the spiritual dimensions of relating to God to how we relate to our physical surroundings. Whereas spiritual righteousness is known through humble service and devotion to God, material righteousness reflects the kingdom's dependence on God. This is represented by the petition in the Lord's Prayer, "Give us this day our daily bread." Jesus' teaching on material matters begins with his warning against storing up treasures on earth instead of in heaven. It ends with his exhortation to concentrate on today's concerns and leave tomorrow's worries until tomorrow. In between he speaks about the eye as the lamp of the body, the impossibility of serving two masters, and the uselessness of worrying about everyday needs.

In the wilderness Jesus had refused the devil's clever and seemingly humane invitation to turn the stones into bread. After forty days and nights without food, such a suggestion would appear entirely appropriate, but Jesus showed no interest in it. Should he have followed his own advice and taken advantage of the "daily bread" he instructs us to request? No. Jesus knew that the economy of God's kingdom was a concept far beyond the self-centered approach the devil was promoting. The incarnate Son of God would not be caught aborting his divine mission on earth. God's righteousness comes as a gift to build up community and to care for all people. It is a strategy neither for personal satisfaction and material accumulation nor for establishing the church as a welfare state. Security for the earthly community of the heavens comes not by searching for protection and stability but by completely depending on the generous, radical blessings of God's kingdom on earth.

The underlying theme for Jesus' revolutionary teaching on the material dimensions of righteousness is found toward the end of this segment: "But seek ye first the kingdom of God, and his righteousness; and all these things shall be added unto you" (6:33 KJV). Those words have become so familiar to many of us that their import can get lost. Just as we noted about the words of the Lord's Prayer, these words have the tendency to take on a separate existence as a song or favorite verse and become detached from their setting in the Sermon on the Mount.

The magnitude of their meaning is underlined by a scarcity of words in the original text, literally translated, "But seek first the kingdom and its righteousness, and all these things will be added to you" (PKC). Ancient manuscripts do not agree on the exact wording, but the more reliable ones do not include the brief phrase "of God" after "seek ye first the kingdom." In the long run, to insert or withdraw "of God" does not change the meaning, but to read the phrase without "of God" sets up a stronger emphasis on the kingdom itself. Certainly the kingdom is God's kingdom, as we know from the context; the previous verse speaks of the community's heavenly Father who knows what they need (as in 6:8). In addition, the Greek word translated as *his* in the phrase "his righteousness" can also be translated just as well as the word *its*. That leaves us with the possible phrase, "But seek first the kingdom and its righteousness." That reading does not change the final meaning of the verse, but tightens it, accenting the righteousness that inhabits the community of God on earth, the kingdom of the heavens. God is the source of that righteousness, to be sure, but God's righteousness is incarnated in the fellowship of God's people. And it is through that kingdom that "all these things shall be added unto you [plural]."

Starting at 6:19 Jesus begins with three short illustrations: storing up treasures, the eye as the body's lamp, and the impossibility of serving two masters. All three relate to righteousness in material things by comparing the self-centered way to the kingdom way. Jesus made the same kind of comparison in his discussion of the spiritual dimensions of righteousness (6:1-6, 16-18), and will do the same with the social dimensions (7:1-12). It is clear that self-centeredness was a human weakness in Jesus' time, just as it is today. The Reverend Bernice A. King, who writes and lectures on life, society, and the world, points this out.

> There are three wicked, evil spirits in the world today:
> (1) Arrogance, (2) selfishness, and (3) materialism and greed. . . .
>
> Arrogance is the belief you are better than anyone else. . . . It is the practice of promoting one's self above all others and exploiting others for personal gain. . . .
>
> Selfishness is saying bad things to others. Selfishness is doing harmful things to others. Selfishness is ignoring humanity for self-promotion.
>
> Materialism and greed is all about money. . . . It's not wrong to have money, but "there's something wrong when you worship money and make it an idol."[2]

I find it interesting and of no surprise that King's "three wicked, evil spirits" relates to the content of Jesus' teaching on the spiritual, material, and social dimensions of righteousness. What King calls "arrogance" we observed in the hypocrites who trumpet their donations and pray long prayers while cheating widows; what King calls "selfishness" we see in the self-centeredness of those who judge others and force their own way (7:1-12); and what King calls "materialism and greed" we see in our topic at hand, in those who store up earthly treasures while ignoring those who need help. Jesus knew what he was talking about. Self-absorption always shows up as opposition to the kingdom way.

As the people of the United States collectively suffered following the shock of 9/11, some greedy citizens took unlawful advantage of the situation. The *Erie* (Pennsylvania) *Times-News* reported on August 6, 2002, that police were investigating thousands of people for using ATMs to steal fifteen million dollars from a New York employees' credit union, whose computer security system was damaged in the attacks. Surely few of those thieves were below the poverty level and desperately needed that money just to exist. Our world worships material wealth and its clout. Television commercials describe the necessity of owning a luxury car and promise that it will fulfill needs we did not know we had. We want to be the one who dies with the most toys. We want to be the one with the most power and prestige, and we'll buy it if we can't get it any other way.

That's a far cry from Jesus' gentle, directing words on how we are to pray: "Give us this day our daily bread." With that prayer we are reminded again that the petition arises from the community, not from our individual, self-focused lives. And we see again that such a prayer assumes our humble day-to-day living, not our concern for financial investments and retirement accounts. By teaching that prayer, Jesus conveys the character of the kingdom of the heavens—what it means to live now as God's people. But, we ask, when Jesus speaks of storing up treasures in heaven, isn't he talking about investing for the future? That's true only if we think of heaven only as that place of reward somewhere and sometime in the hereafter. But heaven already exists, and God's people comprise the kingdom of the heavens, an outpost of heaven that displays the goodness of heaven among people on earth. *Heaven* in 6:19-21 certainly includes the future place and condition God has prepared for committed disciples, but it also includes the heaven that exists now, since heaven is eternal. So to "store up for yourselves treasures in heaven" instead of on earth is presented as the way to choose kingdom values in contrast to acquiring earthly belongings that "moth and rust destroy" and that "thieves break in and steal." Serving God is not to be confused with serving money (6:24), the false god of riches, wealth, and worldly gain, for "ye cannot serve God and mammon" (KJV). The righteousness of the kingdom does not consist of a specific substance that can be saved or a specific act that can be proved. If you fix your eyes on the goodness of heaven, says Jesus, then that is where you will invest yourself—and that will be within the kingdom of the heavens.

To further his point, Jesus refers to the eye that is healthy or unhealthy, sound or unsound. He calls the eye "the lamp of the body," not the "lens" of the body. Ancient peoples regarded the eye not as a window through which light entered but as a lamp that projected light.[3] Eyes were regarded as good or evil, meaning generous or stingy, and represented the person's character: the "lamp" projects what is in the body. Proverbs 22:9 depicts a person who is literally "generous of eye": "He who has a generous eye will be blessed, for he gives of his bread to the poor" (NKJV). And Proverbs 28:22 depicts a person who is literally "stingy of eye": "The stingy [of eye] are eager to get rich and are unaware that poverty awaits them" (TNIV).

So the healthy eye represents persons who are generous with their time, energy, and worldly goods. They are not stingy, as represented by persons with unhealthy eyes. The "lamps" of those who are considerate and benevolent shine brightly because their bodies are "full of light." They fuel their lamps on the kingdom values housed within. They store up heavenly treasures and know what it means to pray, "Give us this day our daily bread." But the "lamps" of those who are selfish and miserly give no light, because their bodies are "full of darkness." There is no kingdom fuel within. They store up earthly treasures and set their hearts on themselves. Jesus says, "If your eye is good, your whole being will radiate the light of God's righteousness; but if your eye is evil, your whole being will know only darkness, and you will waste away into woeful worthlessness" (PKC).

The trio of illustrations closes with the example of a loyal servant who is bound faithfully to one master. No one, says Jesus, can serve two masters. The servant must choose between masters, because the servant's devotion will go to only one, not both. In the context of the Sermon on the Mount, we must choose either the kingdom of the heavens or the kingdom of the world. Either we set our sights on the goodness of heaven or we selfishly look to our own interests. "Ye cannot serve God and mammon" (6:24 KJV).

Jesus follows with his gentle, down-to-earth, picturesque description of God's care.

> Why worry about everyday things like food and drink and clothes? Isn't it obvious that if God nourishes the common birds around you and creates wildflowers of unsurpassed beauty, that this same God would know how to take care of you too? Even you with only the tiniest little faith should know this. (6:25-30 PKC)

After his warnings about storing up treasures on earth instead of in heaven, about being miserly with our possessions instead of generous, and about serving ourselves instead of God, we welcome Jesus' much-needed encouragement and guidance. To accomplish his bidding we need to place our trust in the one who truly cares about our life. To do otherwise is not the kingdom way. It is pagans who worry about material things and strive for them. But people of the kingdom seek first the kingdom and its righteousness, and all the daily things come naturally as part of kingdom life. It is not our business to be struggling to provide everyday needs. That's God's business. People who do not know God struggle and compete to fill their daily needs. They do not know that God, through the kingdom of the heavens, provides what is needed. If we depend on God to "give us this day our daily bread," we have everything we really need. And if we try to store up God's goodness for ourselves, it will rot like stored-up manna.

Ron Kraybill, a professor of conflict transformation, challenges the church to make room for God to heal a broken world. When we fear for our security, we generally don't think in terms of kindness, but we find whatever protection we can: more walls, more weapons, all-out war on those who threaten us. Then the brothers and sons of those we fought against seek retaliation with violence, pushing our response to more missiles and bombs until the destruction of humanity becomes likely. Is there a way that such a vicious cycle of violence could be brought to an end? Kraybill makes a plea for depending on God's security as we respond from within God's righteousness:

> Some three thousand people died of terrorist action on September 11, 2001. But since that time, over twenty million people have died from malnutrition and lack of health care. Surely God cares as much about these deaths as about those who died of terrorist attacks? Why then are we fixated on such a small proportion of human suffering?
>
> If we shifted our focus from "national security" to "human security" we would at last begin to make space for God to work. God's security arises from long-term faithfulness—and in the end it is the only realistic security available. It comes not from the strength of weapons, but from the fruits of doing that which is right.[4]

Worldwide response to the unfathomable destruction and loss in the 2004 tsunami underlines Kraybill's point. When such a colossal tragedy occurs, it affects the whole world, and we get a glimpse of what kingdom goodness can do. Since the tsunami, additional natural disasters have struck around the world: Indonesia's major earthquake and Hurricane Katrina, to name only two. At such times people reach beyond national identity to form a human lifeline, and we don't respond to such desperate human need because of rules and regulations. Our human answer to such calamity often comes beyond and in spite of laws that govern budget responsibilities and international relationships.

What if people around the world were to take that as a picture of how nations might relate to each other even when there is no cataclysmic need? In Bogotá, Colombia, amid hunger and violence, people sing around their dinner table: "Lord, to those who hunger, give bread. And to us who have bread, give the hunger for justice" (English translation). In the kingdom of the heavens, the goodness of God wants to flow through us, blessing others around us.

Jeffrey Sachs, a highly regarded economist and director of the Earth Institute at Columbia University, says that extreme poverty kills twenty thousand people per day, but we don't read those headlines in our daily newspapers. In *The End of Poverty: Economic Possibilities for Our Time* (Penguin Press, 2005), he outlines a plan to eliminate extreme poverty from the world by 2025. Basing his ideas on professional analyses and practical experience in many countries, Sachs says such a goal is possible if the world's wealthiest countries and individuals were to provide even the smallest financial aid. Possible? We do know that we are capable of caring for one another around the world, but we need to be shown the way on an ongoing basis. And the kingdom of the heavens knows how that can happen.

Jesus tells a striking parable:

> Then [Jesus] said, "Beware! Don't be greedy for what you don't have. Real life is not measured by how much we own."
>
> And he gave an illustration: "A rich man had a fertile farm that produced fine crops. In fact, his barns

were full to overflowing. So he said, 'I know! I'll tear down my barns and build bigger ones. Then I'll have room enough to store everything. And I'll sit back and say to myself, My friend, you have enough stored away for years to come. Now take it easy! Eat, drink, and be merry!'

"But God said to him, 'You fool! You will die this very night. Then who will get it all?'

"Yes, a person is a fool to store up earthly wealth but not have a rich relationship with God." (Luke 12:15-21 NLT)

The point of the parable is not that the farmer sinned by building larger barns but that he tried to put his bounteous crops aside for himself. He was looking out for number one. The parable shows what happens when we take a self-centered approach to "our" belongings. In contrast, those who seek the kingdom first always will have enough of what they need because all the members of the kingdom are putting the kingdom first, and "theirs is the kingdom of the heavens"! It is through the kingdom of the heavens that God's righteousness comes. We don't have to worry about food and clothing, since sharing of resources is what kingdom people do. Because the community of the kingdom provides what is needed, God does not need to send manna (at least, not usually!). God blesses kingdom members through each other.

But blessings are blessings only when they are passed along as blessings to others. The rich farmer was blessed with an abundant harvest, but he stopped the flow of God's blessings. And it blew up on him. I sometimes think of the process of blessing in terms of a water system. We are like an empty tank with an inflow valve and an outflow valve. If our outflow valve is closed, the blessings of God soon fill our tank, and we receive no more blessings. But if our outflow valve remains open, God can liberally bless us because there is always room in our tank for more. In the case of the rich farmer, his outflow valve was shut, and God gave him so many blessings that his tank couldn't hold them, and it blew up! If I've received a windfall of money or have found a steady job or enjoy good health, I might say, "God has blessed me." If I really mean that, I will be passing along those blessings in some form to others who are in need of them. Then God can let all blessings flow!

When we hoard our blessings, they become possessions—*our* possessions. Jesus told the young man, "If you want to be perfect, go, sell your possessions and give to the poor, and you will have treasure in [the heavens]. Then come, follow me" (Matthew 19:21 TNIV). Through our church communities, God wants to richly bless the poor in spirit, those who mourn, the meek, those who hunger and thirst for righteousness, the merciful, the pure in heart, the peacemakers, and those who are persecuted because of righteousness. God wants to bless all of us.

After experiencing the shock of 9/11 and gradually coming to a realization of what actually had happened, the people of the United States raised their collective voice. "God Bless America" was followed by "United We Stand" and "Proud of the USA." That unifying and motivating national spirit could only grow as federal and local leaders brought words of comfort and promise to a wounded nation and as innumerable incidents of neighborly care took place person to person in every community around the country. A nation came forward that many people had not seen; a character that had been hidden. Columnists wrote of putting their own priorities in order. Workaholic wage earners promised to spend more time with their families. Neighbors volunteered for community projects. People went back to church.

But the "terrorists" were still out there, and the possibility of additional attacks sent shivers of fear through the nation. War was declared against terrorism and against Iraq and Afghanistan. So just as 9/11 had resulted in a tangible vision of how we might be neighborly to each other, it also pointed out how insecure we felt as a nation, seemingly vulnerable to attacks of any kind at any time. Anthrax scares and terrorism alerts became topics of daily news, and the fear of insecurity began to erode much of what people had gained in being kind to one another. Crimes of selfish greed created havoc in financial companies and became a form of terrorism within our own borders. Rules of constitutional law became hotly contested points of disagreement and anger. Divisions in Christ's church opened into gaping chasms and created an unmerciful war of religion. Instead of the "love your neighbor" attributes that had begun to show, the attributes of "hate your enemy" came back in full force on both the domestic and the international levels.

The kingdom of the heavens blesses everyone around, and when all things are generously shared, there is no need for selfishness. Matthew's story of the birds and wildflowers also appears in the Gospel of Luke, and after Jesus finishes telling it, he says to his listeners: "Do not be afraid, little flock, for your Father is well pleased to give you the kingdom. Sell your possessions and give to the poor" (Luke 12:32-33 NET). God wants to unveil the kingdom! The Father is "well pleased" to give the kingdom to those who commit themselves to God's rule of righteousness.

I can't help but imagine that Jesus delivered this encouragement to his followers with a full and affectionate voice. After all, it was he who had heard the same words from the Father. On his coronation day, Jesus—the Messiah, the beloved Son of God, chosen to fulfill God's eternal plan of salvation—was himself the object of God's delight: "This is my Son, the Beloved, with whom I am well pleased" (Matthew 3:17). Now Jesus in turn joyfully passes along that same, divine benediction to the "little flock." Just as the fullness of God was well pleased to dwell in Jesus, so God's fullness is well pleased to dwell in God's people on earth (see Colossians 1:19; Ephesians 1:22-23; 3:18-19).

The kingdom of the heavens may be upside-down from the world's perspective, but it is right side up in the abundance and generosity of God's righteousness. I've seen it over and over. When God fulfills the focus of a community's prayer—a person saved, an illness healed, a new family in the congregation—my human thinking mistakenly assumes that God's answer is complete, and I thank God for answered prayer. But God doesn't stop at my limits; God always has a generous and loving eye focused on a next step. God's blessings keep on blessing.

A construction manager with Habitat for Humanity in Lima, Ohio, told me that residents of Worth Center, a facility for first-time, nonviolent offenders, sensed the spirit of Christ at the Habitat site where they sometimes worked. "We can't wait till next Wednesday!" they'd say, referring to the day no classes met and they could go out on work assignments. Some said that when they "got out" of the center, they would come back and help Habitat.

Millard and Linda Fuller did not establish Habitat for Humanity to help people be restored to appropriate community citizenship, although they would be pleased for that to happen. They wanted to provide housing for those who needed it, and that was totally right. But God's blessings do not stop at only the first gifts from a "generous eye." In my shortsightedness, I see Habitat houses as a great accomplishment and an answer to prayer. But in God's righteousness, Habitat houses can be more than dwelling places for those who need them. They become steppingstones for myriad blessings of God. In Lima, they have become the training ground for people from the Worth Center. And then what? What is God's next step?

God's blessings do develop in wonderful ways. A mission group from Walnut Hill Mennonite Church in Goshen, Indiana, sought ways to give local youth a constructive response to violence—violence ranging from bullying to school shootings. The group came up with what is a nontraditional answer for a peace church: they adopted the traditions of martial arts that espouse peace and nonviolence. Wes Higginbotham, a church member with a third-degree black belt in Tae Kwon Do, says that threatening situations and interpersonal conflicts often result in "fear, impaired academic performance, diminished self-esteem, counterviolence and suicide." Pastor Steve Thomas, a first-degree black belt instructor, collaborates with Higginbotham to lead a group they call Peacemakers. They teach self-discipline and physical responses to violence that do not require anyone to win or lose. Rather than getting into a cowering stance and raising fists, which invites further aggression, the pastor says, "we teach them to get in a safe stance, get out of harm's way, and have hands ready to block a blow. Keeping a confident stance can diffuse violence."

Because the small mission group of Walnut Hill was faithfully seeking the kingdom and its righteousness, "all these things" they needed were "added unto" them. God's blessings flowed freely through twenty-four local businesses who helped to provide a much-needed space for their ministry. Now located in a 2,200-square-foot academy on Main Street, the Peacemakers use exercises, role plays, and physical training to "talk about God's Spirit and Jesus as the master of peace."[5] Who knows what blessings of God will show up next from this imaginative mission?

The kingdom of our Father in the heavens is known and authenticated when we live out the prayer "Give us this day our daily bread." If that prayer truly represents our seeking first the kingdom of the heavens and its rule of God's righteousness, all our needs are taken care of. Marvelous blessings flow out from God's righteousness, and they come as our *daily* bread. God's desire is to bestow divine blessings on all people, and God wants to do it every day through the kingdom of righteousness. Why should we try to make it any different? Jesus simply says, "Therefore do not worry about tomorrow, for tomorrow will worry about itself. Each day has enough trouble of its own" (6:34 TNIV).

For Discussion

Bill Hybels and Rob Wilkins write that "there is a strangely familiar thread that unites us, an interest we all share: self-interest. Regardless of the continent, the political system, the economic status, the race, it is the universal dark side of humanity: the desire for the last piece of pie, the cause of World War III, the angry hunger in our eyes. It is Me First. This ingrained philosophy of life equates happiness with self-indulgence. It is the belief that power, fame, money, and thrills are the tools we can use to measure success."[6] Compare such self-interest with "material matters" in the kingdom of the heavens.

Sometimes we may think that God too lavishly blesses others. Reflecting on the story of the widow's mite, Madeleine L'Engle writes, "Some unheard-of Elizabethan woman who led a life of selfless love may well be brought before the throne of God ahead of Shakespeare, for such a person may be a greater force for good than someone on whom God's blessings seem to have been dropped more generously."[7] What personal examples can you give to illustrate L'Engle's statement?

How do we know when we have enough? Does it matter? Should it matter?

Social Systems
Feed *What* to the Pigs?

Do not judge, so that you may not be judged. For with the judgment you make you will be judged, and the measure you give will be the measure you get. Why do you see the speck in your neighbor's eye, but do not notice the log in your own eye? Or how can you say to your neighbor, "Let me take the speck out of your eye," while the log is in your own eye? You hypocrite, first take the log out of your own eye, and then you will see clearly to take the speck out of your neighbor's eye.

Do not give what is holy to dogs; and do not throw your pearls before swine, or they will trample them under foot and turn and maul you.

Ask, and it will be given you; search, and you will find; knock, and the door will be opened for you. For everyone who asks receives, and everyone who searches finds, and for everyone who knocks, the door will be opened. Is there anyone among you who, if your child asks for bread, will give a stone? Or if the child asks for a fish, will give a snake? If you then, who are evil, know how to give good gifts to your children, how much more will your Father in [the heavens] give good things to those who ask him!

In everything do to others as you would have them do to you; for this is the law and the prophets. (Matthew 7:1-12)

On May 7, 2004, twenty-six-year-old Nicholas Berg and six others were beheaded in Iraq by Islamic militants in one of those horrible, tragic acts that takes place in war. How does one deal with such shock and loss? How does one respond? In like manner? And how does the family handle such grief? Nicholas's family reached out the following month with this statement presented by his father, Michael:

> We, the family of Nicholas Berg, extend our sympathies to the families of Kim Sun-il, Paul Johnson Jr., Robert Jacobs, Kenneth Scroggs, Bassam Salih Kubba and Kamal al-Jarah. We hope they will find the strength to endure the pain of their losses. We also extend our sympathies to all the families and friends of all the victims of this war, including United States military, other coalition military, contractors, and the 11,000-plus innocent Iraqi victims. We have been silent until now to avoid for the Johnson and Sun-il families any association our son's death may have had.[1]

The November 26, 2004, issue of *National Catholic Reporter* stated that letters of condolence and apology from Muslims helped Michael Berg grieve his loss and that he wanted to reciprocate. His response in part was to support the Iraq Photo Project, sponsored by the Fellowship of Reconciliation, as it sent photos to Iraq of ordinary Americans holding handwritten signs apologizing for the U.S. invasion and occupation. In the spring of 2005, Michael, an avowed atheist, sought out a course on forgiveness at a Catholic college near his home. "Forgiveness was something I had been wrestling with since the moment I got the phone call that Nick was dead," he said. "I had this huge burning fire within me, and I wanted to get rid of it."[2]

The community of Christ is built not only on spiritual devotion to God and a generous attitude about material possessions, but also on gracious social interaction with others. In Matthew 7:1-12 Jesus focuses on how to relate to our neighbors. When we pray as a community, "And forgive us our debts, as we also have forgiven our debtors," we place ourselves in a vulnerable position. We challenge ourselves to live out what we so fervently desire. Forgiveness, as a blessing of God, is received only as it is passed on. That is the kingdom way. To open and close this section on social dimensions, Jesus utilizes proverbs that may be just as familiar outside the church as inside: "Judge not, that you may not be judged," and the so-called golden rule, "Do unto others as you would have them do unto you." They are similar, each containing a mutual interaction that reminds us that no one is alone—that others are involved in whatever we do, and that we are involved in whatever they do.

The direction of focus here adds a new dimension to the directions of the spiritual and material spheres of righteousness. If we use the image of pointer arrows, the arrow for spiritual dimensions points from us to God and the arrow for material dimensions points from us to others. Jesus depicted both of those directions when he answered the lawyer who asked which was the greatest commandment: "You shall love the Lord your God with all your heart, and with all your soul, and with all your mind. This is the greatest and first commandment. And a second is like it: You shall love your neighbor as yourself" (Matthew 22:37-39).

Then on the last night of his earthly sojourn, Jesus added a new, third commandment: "I give you a new commandment—to love one another. Just as I have loved you, you also are to love one another. Everyone will know by this that you are my disciples—if you have love for one another" (John 13:34-35 NET).

That new commandment represents the social sphere. Here the arrow has a point on both ends and points not only from me to others but also *to* me *from* others, indicating purposeful interaction. To love *one another* is foundational. Mutuality in the kingdom of the heavens cannot exist except that we acknowledge "us" instead of "me." It seems so simple, and yet we forget! "Forgive us our debts *as we also* have forgiven our debtors." There is interplay among the members of the community. And blessing that is passed among members of the community affects even those outside the community (maybe, *especially* those outside the community).

When we judge others, we set ourselves apart and above and make ourselves the measure. You've probably heard (or expressed) the saying "Those who drive faster than I do are maniacs. Those who drive slower are idiots." As in all spheres of life, our view of people around us is often self-centered. Jesus cautions that we'll get what we deserve. When he illustrates his warning with the example of the speck of sawdust in our neighbor's eye and the plank in our own, it is appropriate that we think individually. But we must consider the community aspect, as well. In the church today there are divisions within denominations and between mainline and evangelical, conservative and liberal, male and female. Between pro-life and pro-choice, death penalty and no abortion, abortion and no death penalty, heterosexual and homosexual. Between war and no war, war and pro-life, no war and pro-choice, and on and on.

Are we church or not? That is the question. What does it mean when we call ourselves Presbyterian or Mennonite or Catholic or Lutheran? What does it mean when we think of ourselves as Independent or Full Gospel or Methodist or Church of the Nazarene? At best, such titles indicate the elbows, eyes, and toenails of the church that Paul describes in 1 Corinthians 12, all working together smoothly as the body of Christ. At worst, such titles describe judgmental stances we claim against other Christians who may in fact believe in Jesus Christ just as ardently as we do, but with differences. Even within denominations we quash each other with judgmental labels and attitudes, and choose the "correct" stance for ourselves. We think of ourselves as the "true" church, and by our standards we determine who's in and who's out.

But what if we saw our chosen titles for what they are: adjectives instead of nouns? Isn't it true that we are not Baptists, but Baptist *Christians*? Aren't we Quaker *Christians* and Assemblies of God *Christians* and Episcopal Church *Christians*? Could it be that the church is actually receiving the judgmental measure it is giving out? As the world outside the church runs away from the church instead of to it, they are judging the church by how we judge each other inside the church. Pulitzer Prize-winning commentator Leonard Pitts Jr. observes with sorrow that the Christian church appears to be "little more than a refuge for human meanness, pettiness, partisanship and smug self-satisfaction."[3] Why would I want to join a holier-than-thou group of hypocrites who quarrel and fight among themselves but tell me to put my life in order? Wouldn't we rather have the non-church world judge us according to the prayer we regularly pray: "Forgive us our debts as we also have forgiven our debtors"?

Jesus moves on with a parable that advances the point he is making. People do not feed their dogs with meat sacrificed at the temple, any more than they throw pearl jewelry into the pigpen. Neither action is proper, and besides, the pigs would tromp all over the pearls while the wild dogs attacked the people. For many readers, this parable remains obscure, and scholars over the centuries have given it innumerable interpretations. Some treat it only as one of the many interesting sayings Jesus delivered during his ministry, just as they consider the Sermon on the Mount to be an arbitrary collection.

However, we must accept either that Jesus arranged the order of the Sermon to clearly convey his word or that Matthew laid out the sermon to present the meaning of Jesus' message. Frequently, readers relate this giving of sacred things to dogs and throwing of pearls to pigs as foolishly squandering one's fine things on insensitive, unappreciative, uncivilized persons. The common expression "pearls before swine" refers to this parable and generally is taken to mean the wasting of one's breath in trying to impart very important things to unreceptive or belligerent persons. There is some truth to that, as we will see, but the fault does not belong to the unresponsive person. In the preceding verses, Jesus has been teaching about the sinful behavior of judging others for imperfections and failures that show up even worse in ourselves. Given that context, this parable focuses on our inappropriate behavior toward others and the response it provokes.[4]

If we wrongly interpret the references to dogs and pigs as looking down on "barbarians" who wouldn't understand the good we are giving them, that tells us a lot about the log in our own eye. As was widely reported in the media in October 2003, Maryland's first lady, Kendel Ehrlich, told a domestic violence prevention conference, "You know, really, if I had an opportunity to shoot Britney Spears, I think I would." Although she was laughing, and apologized later, the image she projected of herself could be considered "barbarian." Or consider evangelist Jimmy Swaggart, who told the world in his September 12, 2004, sermon that he'd never seen a man he wanted to marry. "And I'm gonna be blunt and plain, if one ever looks at me like that I'm going to kill him and tell God he died." Such coldheartedness, even if in jest, comes at the expense of someone else and raises all kinds of improper thoughts and contempt. In the late 1960s and early 1970s I heard evangelist Tom Skinner recount the hatred that arose in Harlem from what the people there experienced at the hands of those they called racists, who came into Harlem from the outside to establish law and order. In anger the people of Harlem raised their sarcastic cry: "But it's your law for our order!"

Jesus, with his parable about dogs and pigs, puts his finger on this sore spot. From our arrogant position of believing we possess holy words and pearls of wisdom, we easily push our own agenda onto those who don't agree with it or may not be ready for it. When we selfishly think we have the answers without knowing the real questions, it is no wonder that those on whom we force our standards violently turn on us. A book by Edward Lazarus tells the same story, even if we get no further than its title: *Black Hills/White Justice: The Sioux Nation Versus the United States 1775 to the Present.*[5] As nations, as institutions, as churches, and as individuals we tend toward justifying ourselves and condemning others. We think in terms of withholding from unworthy people what we consider to be wonderful treasures of truth and service. Dallas Willard writes,

> The problem with pearls for pigs is not that the pigs are not worthy. It is not worthiness that is in question here at all, but helpfulness. Pigs cannot digest pearls, cannot nourish themselves upon them. Likewise for a dog with a Bible or a crucifix. The dog cannot eat it. The reason these animals will finally "turn and rend you," when one day you step up to them with another load of Bibles or pearls, is that you at least are edible.[6]

How then do we exemplify our petition, "Forgive us our debts as we also have forgiven our debtors"? Jesus continues with words that have become familiar: ask, seek, and knock. People often cite this passage as asking God for whatever we want or need, and if we seek diligently and knock persistently, we will get what we prayed for. But let's put verses 7 and 8 in context. Jesus is teaching about how we treat each other—not judging, not peering out from behind our log to spot someone else's speck of sawdust, not lording it over others with our arrogant, self-centered attitude. Following such explicit examples of how *not to* relate to each other, Jesus now teaches us *how to* relate to each another. Instead of telling, we ask. Instead of presuming, we seek. Instead of forcing, we knock. "For everyone who asks receives [in the kingdom of the heavens]; those who seek find [in the kingdom of the heavens]; and to those who knock, the door will be opened [in the kingdom of the heavens]" (Matthew 7:8 TNIV).

Asking, seeking, and knocking are characteristics of the kingdom of the heavens. As attributes of that community, surely those characteristics are bound to spill out into relationships with those who are not part of the kingdom community. We may not expect non-kingdom people to respond in like manner, but they might. Asking, seeking, and knocking are attractive qualities, and whether or not others embrace those features, some certainly will see that God's goodness abides in those disciples who love one another in such a way.

The April 2003 *Parade Magazine* ran a story on fighting terrorism with something other than war. Documented by innumerable news accounts, the tale of Greg Mortenson and the people of the small Pakistani village of Korphe illustrates the principle of "ask, seek, and knock." In 1993 Mortenson, an emergency-room nurse from San Francisco and a former U.S. Army medic, was climbing the world's second-tallest mountain in one of the world's most volatile war zones. He became ill and stumbled down the mountain, walking five days to the nearest village, where people took him into their home and nursed him back to health. As he began to know them Mortenson saw that the village's eighty-four children had no teacher and were writing with sticks in the sand. Touched by the villagers' kindness, he vowed to return and pay them back by building a school and providing a teacher's endowment.

Another of Mortenson's motivations for establishing the tiny four-room school was his hope that education through secular schools would help to lessen people's support for the Taliban and other extremist sects. He says,

> We've spent billions of dollars building a wall around America with homeland security, but we also need to reach out to build bridges. . . . If we try to resolve terrorism with military might and nothing else, then we will be no safer than we were before 9/11. In the long-term, we have to help feed and clothe people where

terrorists are recruiting volunteers. And we have to educate them—especially the girls. We have to prove to them that the world can be a better place. If we truly want a legacy of peace for our children, we need to understand that this is a war that will ultimately be won with books, not with bombs.[7]

What started as a difficult and often lonely quest by Mortenson has grown into Central Asia Institute, a nonprofit organization that welcomes community participation and whose projects are locally initiated. Since that first school in September 1996, fifty-five more have been built in the region. The organization has successfully completed more than one hundred community projects in northern Pakistan's Karakoram Mountains. The full story, as told by Mortenson and David Oliver Relin in *Three Cups of Tea* (Viking, 2006), has caught enough people's imagination to loft it onto the *New York Times* Best Sellers list. When people together "ask, seek, and knock," nonfunctional and competing social systems can come tumbling down.

After Jesus interpreted the ancient law of "an eye for an eye, and a tooth for a tooth" and had given examples of how to respond to those who mistreat you or force you to do something for them, he went on to add, "Give to those who ask, and don't turn away from those who want to borrow" (5:42 NLT). That's the way kingdom people treat others. It's simple. Everyone is included. It's a community of mutuality. Ask, seek, knock—and *give* to those who ask, seek, and knock. But that takes humility. John Ortberg voices our confession: "There is a self-righteousness in me that does not want to die. There is something inside me that is not bothered when others are excluded, that wants others to be excluded, that feels more special when I'm on the inside and somebody else is not."[8]

As a pastor, how do I interact with other kingdom members? Am I above them or better than they are or maybe in a more favored position? When I preach, teach, and visit, my word may mistakenly be thought of as more important than that of others in the Christian community. But am I the church? Do I run the church? Do I alone place people in their responsibilities of service? How does a pastor ask, seek, and knock? If Jesus means what he says about the kingdom, my voice and presence are not more important than anyone else's, just different. All kingdom people respond to God's call for them to serve in the ministries for which they have been gifted. I too have committed my life to the work of the kingdom and have prepared God's gifts in me to the best of my ability.

Beyond that, I have been charged and set aside for the specific ministry I do. It is important that I take seriously my responsibilities as spiritual director and representative of the congregation. But all of that does not elevate me to a place where I am above others, where I can hear God's word better than they do or where the insights, interests, and visions of others are less important. Nor does it give me license to force my ideas onto them and run a one-man show.

It is clear as well that the community prayer must always be my confession: "And forgive us our debts, as we also have forgiven our debtors." One of my greatest satisfactions as a pastor has been to see members of the church come to the point where they know they are the church—not just puppets of the pastor—and are enjoying it. Jesus tells us not to judge others as if we are on the top. Let everyone in the community be an integral part of its essence. That's the kingdom way.

Jesus follows immediately with the illustration of giving good things to our children. Even though we are evil, we have that parent-child bond that guides parents into knowing how to give good, appropriate things to sons and daughters. If that is true on the human level, says Jesus, even though we are evil, think how much more it is true between the Father in the heavens and the children of the kingdom. Do we find it difficult to ask each other's opinion, preferring our own while we show no interest in what others say? Do we imagine that only we have the right answers, hesitating to seek out what others think, not wanting to share the credit if they come up with something similar? And, rather than inquiring whether we might join in cooperation with others, do we force our beliefs on them, not even wanting to be associated with them? Often we prefer judging others, looking down on their specks of imperfection while we dictate our high and mighty demands. Jesus says that the kingdom of the heavens operates on the principle of mutuality, that the entire social interaction of the community is beautifully affected by God's righteousness. And the holy God, the Father in the heavens who knows what we need (see 6:8, 32), gives the good gift of righteousness to the children of the kingdom—if only we ask, seek, and knock.

Jesus wraps up his lesson on the social sphere of life with the golden rule: "Do unto others as you would have them do unto you." As a saying, it can stand on its own, but in the original language, verse 12 is connected to what goes before with the conjunction *so*, or *therefore*—meaning, taking all of this into account, do this. Doing unto others as you would have them do to you means that the mutuality of the kingdom of the heavens expresses God's righteousness. And the proverb gives an easy handle to remember that important, essential truth. In the community of Christ, members are vulnerable before one another, loving each other as God loved us in Christ. Do you want to experience that? Then live it! From the letter to the Ephesians, these verses masterfully pinpoint the mutuality of the Christian church:

> Put away from you all bitterness and wrath and anger
> and wrangling and slander, together with all malice,
> and be kind to one another, tenderhearted, forgiving
> one another, as God in Christ has forgiven you.
> Therefore be imitators of God, as beloved children,
> and live in love, as Christ loved us and gave himself

up for us, a fragrant offering and sacrifice to God. (4:31-5:2)

Jesus is not quite done with this portion of his sermon, however, and to the end of the golden rule he adds, "for this is the law and the prophets." To sharpen the word *is*, some versions say "fulfills" or "sums up," but the Greek simply says "is," which is actually stronger: there is no question—this is what the law and the prophets say. But in addition here we see the skillful double use of "the law and the prophets." Not only does it suitably conclude Jesus' teaching on the social dimensions of righteousness, but it also brings to a close the larger, major body of Jesus' teaching in the Sermon on the Mount in which he has taught the validity, meaning, and practical application of God's law (see 5:17—7:12). In 5:17, after announcing the kingdom of the heavens, Jesus had said, "Do not think that I have come to abolish the law or the prophets." Now he says in conclusion, "for this is the law and the prophets."

In response to the lawyer who asked which was the greatest commandment, Jesus had told him to "love the Lord your God with all your heart, and with all your soul, and with all your mind" and to "love your neighbor as yourself." In the next verse, Jesus continued, "On these two commandments hang all the law and the prophets" (Matthew 22:40). But the fulfillment of the law through Jesus goes beyond the law and the prophets—not in contrast to them or to abolish them, but to fulfill them. The late Clarence Bauman wrote, "In his life and thought Jesus was entirely absorbed with the written Torah of the Old Testament and frequently quoted from the Pentateuch, from the major and minor prophets, and from the Psalter. On the strength of this identity with the written Law, Jesus deepened its demands, thereby fulfilling its intention in a radical way."[9]

On the day of resurrection, Jesus joined two people on their way to Emmaus and showed them how the law and the prophets spoke about him (see Luke 24:25-27). A few days

earlier, on the night he was betrayed, Jesus had told his disciples that to live beyond the law meant that they were to love
not only God and their neighbor, but also one another (see
John 13:34-35).

> Pray, Jesus says to the community,
>> that God's kingdom may come among you as it
>> is in heaven;
>> that God may sustain your daily needs; and
>> that God may forgive you as you forgive each
>> other.

For Discussion

In 1906 the enigmatic Ambrose Bierce wrote *Cynic's
Work Book*, later to become *Devil's Dictionary*, which since
has appeared in numerous published versions. Bierce defines
an evangelist as "a bearer of good tidings, particularly (in a
religious sense) such as assure us of our own salvation and the
damnation of our neighbors." Was he right? How does that
view compare with "ask (don't tell), seek (don't presume) and
knock (don't force)," as applied in your congregation, and in
the larger world?

Use the following prayer as an example for writing similar prayers: "Our Father in the heavens, help us remember
that the jerk who cut us off in traffic last night is a single
mother who worked nine hours yesterday and was rushing
home to cook dinner, help with homework, do the laundry,
and spend a few precious moments with her children."

Some clever pundit noted that there seems to be a new
golden rule in Congress: "It's not whether you win or lose, it's
how you lay the blame." I'm glad that law is stuck in com-
mittee. How about you?

Fruits and Faithfulness
A Word to the Wise
—and the Foolish

Enter through the narrow gate; for the gate is wide and the road is easy that leads to destruction, and there are many who take it. For the gate is narrow and the road is hard that leads to life, and there are few who find it.

Beware of false prophets, who come to you in sheep's clothing but inwardly are ravenous wolves. You will know them by their fruits. Are grapes gathered from thorns, or figs from thistles? In the same way, every good tree bears good fruit, but the bad tree bears bad fruit. A good tree cannot bear bad fruit, nor can a bad tree bear good fruit. Every tree that does not bear good fruit is cut down and thrown into the fire. Thus you will know them by their fruits.

Not everyone who says to me, "Lord, Lord," will enter the kingdom of [the heavens], but only the one who does the will of my Father in [the heavens]. On that day many will say to me, "Lord, Lord, did we not prophesy in your name, and cast out demons in your name, and do many deeds of power in your name?" Then I will declare to them, "I never knew you; go away from me, you evildoers."

Everyone then who hears these words of mine and acts on them will be like a wise man who built his house on rock. The rain fell, the floods came, and the winds blew and beat on that house, but it did not fall, because it had been founded on rock. And everyone who hears these words of mine and does not act on them will be like a foolish man who built his house on sand. The rain fell, and the floods came, and the winds blew and beat against that house, and it fell— and great was its fall! (Matthew 7:1-12)

"Enter," Jesus says. "Come into the kingdom of the heavens through the narrow gate" (7:13). At the beginning of his Sermon, Jesus had announced that the kingdom of the heavens—prophesied by John the Baptist and proclaimed by himself (see 3:2; 4:17)—was already here. It welcomes everyone, he said, common people included, not just the religious elite (see 5:3-16). Then he moved to the major portion of his Sermon, 5:17—7:12, in which he confirmed that God's law of righteousness is valid and that it is to be obeyed when interpreted in light of God's eternal goodness. But, more than that, God's law is to be applied to the practical, everyday life of those who choose to live in the kingdom of the heavens. Now to close his sermon, Jesus warns his listeners that there are dangers along the way to kingdom life (7:13-20) and spells out the entrance requirements to the kingdom (7:21-27). In 5:11-16 Jesus had announced mutuality as an attractive and prominent feature of the kingdom, and here in 7:13-20 he shows how that relationship can be destroyed by self-serving people. With the Beatitudes (5:3-10) Jesus had declared the acceptance and blessing of all people from all walks of life, and here in 7:21-27, although everyone is welcome in the kingdom, Jesus gives a basic requirement that must be met by those who desire to enter.

Throughout, Jesus already has raised some red flags, and they are not to be taken lightly. In 5:20 he stated that people cannot enter the kingdom of the heavens unless their righteousness goes beyond that of the scribes and Pharisees. In his brief commentary on forgiveness, which follows the Lord's Prayer, Jesus warned that our heavenly Father will not forgive us unless we forgive others (see 6:15). In his teaching on the material dimensions of righteousness in 6:23, Jesus explained that we have a great darkness inside us if we approach the world with a stingy eye. And in 7:2 he noted that we will be judged in the same way that we judge. The dire consequence of not following the law of God's righteousness is in all cases predictable: we miss out on the kingdom of the heavens. And now, in 7:13-14, with his parable of the wide and narrow gates, Jesus laments that not only will we miss out on the kingdom if we take the wrong path, but we will end up on the road to destruction.

Getting into the kingdom of the heavens is not easy, Jesus warns, and only a few get in. But, we ask, doesn't that contradict his generous welcome announced to everyone from all categories of life? No, there is no contradiction. Everyone is welcome and invited, but Jesus is stating the unfortunate, obvious fact: many people, he observes, are more interested in their own pursuits than in the life of the kingdom. "Oh," I say, "I definitely want the benefits of the kingdom. But does that mean I have to give up my own kingdom? Why can't I have both? I try to live the life of the kingdom (even go to church!) by trying to make the life of the kingdom come alive in me. Right?" Sorry, but that's backward, and there are major obstacles in that path. Rather, my life needs to come alive through the life of the kingdom. I can't make the kingdom come alive in me. Jesus said, "But seek first the kingdom and its righteousness, and all these things will be added to you [plural]" (6:33 PKC). The only alternative is destruction.

What does that mean? What does it mean to be on the road to eternal destruction? In his third discourse, Jesus describes such a downfall with the vivid and mysterious language of yet another parable:

> Once again, the kingdom of [the heavens] is like a net
> that was let down into the lake and caught all kinds of
> fish. When it was full, the fishermen pulled it up on the
> shore. Then they sat down and collected the good fish
> in baskets, but threw the bad away. This is how it will
> be at the end of the age. The angels will come and sep-
> arate the wicked from the righteous and throw them
> into the blazing furnace, where there will be weeping
> and gnashing of teeth. (Matthew 13:47-50 TNIV)

Just as the kingdom of the heavens is already present with
us, the kingdom of evil is already present too. Just as the blessings of God's kingdom on earth are here, though not in their
fullness, the "blazing furnace" and the "weeping and gnashing
of teeth" are here too, though not in their fullness. Or is that
too painfully obvious? Is it possible that the greed, selfishness,
and arrogance we experience on a day-to-day basis represent
the kingdom of evil? They certainly do not belong to the kingdom of the heavens. Is it possible that the spiritual impoverish-
ment of much of Christ's church represents the kingdom of evil?
It certainly does not belong to the kingdom of the heavens. Is it
possible that the atrocities of war represent the kingdom of evil?
They certainly do not belong to the kingdom of the heavens.
Isn't it true that just as there can be heaven on earth, there can
be hell on earth? Isn't it true that whoever does not belong to
the kingdom of the heavens belongs to the kingdom of evil? In
John 3:16 and its following commentary, that very contrast of
kingdoms is identified. Note that the noun *destruction* of
Matthew 7:13 ("the road that leads to destruction") comes
from the same Greek root as the verb *perish* in John 3:16.

> For God so loved the world that he gave his only Son,
> so that everyone who believes in him will not perish
> but have eternal life. God did not send his Son into the
> world to condemn it, but to save it. There is no judg-
> ment awaiting those who trust him. But those who do
> not trust him have already been judged for not believ-
> ing in the only Son of God. Their judgment is based

on this fact: The light from heaven came into the world, but they loved the darkness more than the light, for their actions were evil. They hate the light because they want to sin in the darkness. They stay away from the light for fear their sins will be exposed and they will be punished. But those who do what is right come to the light gladly, so everyone can see that they are doing what God wants. (John 3:16-21 NLT)

In Matthew 7:13-14 Jesus says that those who choose the wide gate and the easy road will perish. Many enter that road; they take it by default. But—and I like the contrast—the few that are on the road that leads to life *find* it. They look for it and find it.

Beginning at 7:15, Jesus also warns that when self-centered, power-hungry people manipulate the kingdom of the heavens for their own benefit, they destroy its mutuality and bring themselves to a calamitous end. They have not learned that the blessings of the kingdom are to flow through them to enrich everyone around them. How do we recognize these "false prophets" who come disguised as gentle sheep, improperly dispensing the duties of the kingdom to satisfy their own desires? If a grape grows on thorns, you know something is wrong, and something is out of whack if thistles produce a fig. In the same way, something is wrong if a local church looks down its Pinocchio nose at corruption in the neighborhood, while members of the church squabble among themselves about worship styles. Something is out of whack if a church preaches generosity to the poor but spends its money mainly on its pastor and on its buildings and promotions. And what if the pastor's word is law, and no one in the congregation is permitted to raise a different perspective or to question anything that comes from behind the pulpit? Are not all members of a congregation invited and expected to use their God-given gifts wherever those gifts are needed? Or are some categories of people not valued or "qualified"?

Jesus says we'll know "false prophets" by their fruit, because it's like trees bearing fruit. Fruit can identify healthy, attractive life or improper, deadly behavior. In the parable about trees and fruit, the Bible's original language uses two different words for "good" and two for "bad." The King James Version picks up on these nuances and orients the parable toward its spiritual interpretation: "Even so every good tree bringeth forth good fruit; but a corrupt tree bringeth forth evil fruit. A good tree cannot bring forth evil fruit, neither *can* a corrupt tree bring forth good fruit. Every tree that bringeth not forth good fruit is hewn down, and cast into the fire. Wherefore by their fruits ye shall know them" (7:17-20 KJV).

If the tree is good (righteous), fruit produced by that tree comes from God's goodness. If the tree is bad (unrighteous), fruit produced by that tree comes from evil (or the evil one). No fruit can cause its tree to be good or bad. In the same way, righteousness flows from God, not from what we do for God. Obeying the law does not make us righteous. The law of God's righteousness can be fulfilled in us only as we abide in the goodness of God, just as a branch can bear good fruit only as it abides in the vine that is Christ (see John 15:1-10).

In the New Testament there are descriptions of behavior that we view as codes of law for the church, lists of do's and don'ts. Many times the church takes them as laws to be fulfilled and uses them as strict rules to be obeyed. But if we concentrate only on the quality of the fruit—whether it is good or bad, or whether we have obeyed the rules or not—our lives are centered on trying to do something good, and we work by our own might and power to achieve it. If a church, a pastor, or any individual is bad or self-centered—unrighteous—they cannot become good—righteous—by doing good deeds or obeying laws. The apostle Paul says that if you are led by the Spirit, you will produce the fruit of the Spirit. If you are led by gratification of the flesh, you will produce bad fruit. He urges us to keep in step with the Spirit (see Galatians 5:16-26). If we abide in Christ and welcome the Holy Spirit to live among us, the good tree bears good fruit.

So how do we get into the kingdom of the heavens? Jesus has told us it is open to everyone and exists for everyone and invites everyone to join, no matter their station in life—ethnic background, nationality, religious standing, financial standing, social standing, vocation, gender, age, place of residence. But there remains a basic requirement for getting in. Jesus says that not every person who calls him Lord will enter the kingdom of the heavens: "Not all people who sound religious are really good" (7:21 NLT). Not all people who go to church or carry Bibles or lead church projects or say they are born again are permitted in. "Knowing the correct password—saying 'Master, Master,' for instance—isn't going to get you anywhere with me" (Msg).

"The only entrance requirement for the kingdom of the heavens," says Jesus, "is to do the will of my Father in the heavens" (PKC).

In my weakness I want to respond to Jesus' clear, momentous statement with delaying tactics. I want to answer like the expert in the law who tried to trick him. In Luke's version of the story, the lawyer asks Jesus what he needs to do to inherit eternal life.

To this Jesus answers, "What do you read in the law of Moses?"

The expert recites, "You shall love the LORD your God with all your heart, with all your soul, with all your strength, and with all your mind, and your neighbor as yourself" (Luke 10:27 NKJV).

Jesus confirms his answer: "Do that, and you will live."

But then the lawyer responds in weakness, trying to justify himself: "And who is my neighbor?" (Luke 10:29 NKJV).

One good result of the lawyer's crafty protest was Jesus' timeless story of the good Samaritan. But the lawyer's devious question expressed the typical, human response to the straightforward message of Jesus. And, sadly, his response comes too close for comfort in illustrating my own weakness.

When Jesus says that the only entrance requirement for the kingdom of the heavens is to do the will of his Father in the heavens, I, in my weakness, want to say craftily, "And what *is* the will of your Father?" As if Jesus had not just spent his entire sermon describing the life of God's kingdom. As if Jesus had not just validated God's law of righteousness, interpreted it, and applied it to everyday life. As if Jesus himself did not practice what he preached. But I am too secure, too comfortable, too sure in my own grasp of the written law and in my subjection to the rules. I can't cut loose and allow God's holy will to guide God's own community on earth as it is in heaven and to carry me along in that refreshing stream.

The Bible says that when the expert in the law asked, "And who is my neighbor," he wanted to justify himself. The Greek word for "justify" has the same root as the word translated *righteous*. The lawyer tried to imply that he was acting out of righteousness, that he had a pure spirit. How sad. And how familiar such a sneaky response sounds today. I can even appear religious while lying, "And what *would* Jesus do?" As if I didn't already know.

In his Sermon Jesus predicts that he will meet resistance "on that day." Those many people who don't get into the kingdom will say, "But, Lord, how can you refuse us? Can't you see how righteous we are? Didn't you see what we did? We preached great messages about you—in your name! We even confronted the powers of evil, showing your might through us. And we displayed all the evidence of your divine power so that people would know your name. We, we, we . . ." (Matthew 7:22 PKC). The scene is much like the one that appears in the larger story of Matthew 25:31-46, the ending of Jesus' fifth discourse. There the Son of man separates the people of all nations as a shepherd separates the sheep from the goats. The sheep are "the blessed," those who inherit the kingdom prepared for them by the Father. The goats are "the cursed," those who are sent away into the everlasting fire prepared for the devil and his angels. When the king tells the goats what will happen to them, they raise an angry cry.

Earlier the king had told the sheep where they were headed, and they were surprised by such a wonderful gift: "How do we deserve this?" The Lord answered that they had served him while serving all those who were in need. (In terms of the Sermon on the Mount, the sheep had announced the generous welcome of the kingdom of the heavens and had passed on its blessings.) But now the goats were angry. They had heard what the king had told "the righteous," and the goats thought they too should receive a great reward, since they definitely had done high-profile things for others. John Fischer spots the paradox: "One of the ironic similarities between heaven and hell is that no one in either place thinks they got what they deserve."[1]

Like the would-be chef with the newest and best cookware, like the mediocre band with the most impressive sound equipment and lights, and like the best-dressed golfer with the latest clubs and highest score, the goats miss the point. "We were always doing good things," they wail. But the Lord tells them, "Yes, but you were not serving me!" The story ends with the sobering, decisive words: "And these shall go away into everlasting punishment: but the righteous into life eternal" (Matthew 25:46 KJV).

Some years ago when my daughter, Judy, and her family were living near my late mother-in-law, Judy would take her little son and infant daughter for visits. Although Nancy and I were living a great distance away, we did not need to require Judy to do that. She and her husband were following no rule that said they were supposed to take their children to see Great-Grandma every week or every two weeks or whatever. They went to eat with her, to enjoy her presence, to learn from her, to play games, and to do what families do. I can't imagine how badly Nancy and I would have felt if we had had to require Judy and her family to visit Great-Grandma or even to remind them to do so. And they weren't trying to impress anybody. They went to visit her because that is what they did naturally as family. The kingdom of the heavens is like that. It is not by law that we carry out the attributes of the kingdom but by the goodness that makes us children in God's family.

Jesus declares that not all those who say to him, "Lord, Lord," will enter the kingdom of the heavens. And like the "goats" of Matthew 25, these self-righteous people get angry too: "Why don't we get in?" they wail. "We did everything right!" Then Jesus answers with one of the saddest comments in the Bible: "I never knew you" (7:23). How surprising, and embarrassing—"I never knew you." We identify with those people; we feel their pain. "What do you mean, Jesus, 'I never knew you'? We did all those things! We followed all the rules!" But self-righteous people can't see, don't know. We plan to enter the kingdom of the heavens by accomplishing good things to make us good, instead of by knowing Christ. To know Christ is to be blessed by righteousness from God so that God's goodness can flow through us. We cannot make ourselves good or righteous. We must admit such a truth if we are to do the will of the Father in the heavens. Our righteousness needs to go beyond that of the scribes and the Pharisees, or we will never enter the kingdom of the heavens (see 5:20).

To know someone in the sense Jesus uses here is to know someone completely. It is the same word (Greek: *ginosko*) used in the biblical sense of husbands and wives knowing each other intimately. Matthew 1:25 says that Joseph "did not know [Mary] till she had brought forth her firstborn Son" (NKJV). Jesus' knowledge of us does not consist of facts he's dug up somewhere or of personal records stored away like credits and debits in a judgment-day ledger. His knowing of us is based on a relationship with us.

In his words to the disciples in the upper room, Jesus compares the incomplete knowing of servants with the complete knowing of friends, made possible by God through Jesus.

> "You are my friends if you do what I command. I no longer call you servants, because servants do not know their master's business. Instead, I have called you friends, for everything that I learned from my Father I have made known to you. You did not choose me, but I chose you and appointed you so that you might go and bear fruit—fruit that will last—and so that whatever you ask in my name the Father will give you." (John 15:14-16 TNIV).

The image of bearing fruit recalls what Jesus said about spotting false prophets: "You will know them by their fruits" (7:16, 20). Good fruits come from good trees. Good fruits cannot come from bad trees. When the self-righteous people cry, "Look what we did!" Jesus knows that their fruit is bad, because it comes from bad trees. And he says, "I never knew you."

When we pray, "Your will be done, on earth as it is in heaven," we would do well to add the confession that we cannot do it ourselves, either as individuals or as a community. It is done by God through us. The writer of 1 John is clear: "If we say we do not bear the guilt of sin, we are deceiving ourselves and the truth is not in us. But if we confess our sins, [God] is faithful and righteous, forgiving us our sins and cleansing us from all unrighteousness" (1:8-9 NET).

For Jesus to know us, it is up to us to meet him face to face. Jesus already gave of himself to accomplish the will of the Father in the heavens. Now it is our turn. Who would ever want to hear those joyless words from Jesus: "I never knew you"?

When Jesus tells the arrogant people, "I never knew you," he doesn't stop there. In the same breath he continues: "Go away from me, you evildoers" (7:23). Not only have the self-righteous not carried out the will of the Father in the heavens, they also have done evil. How disturbing! To be called an evildoer would make me even angrier. What the protesters had perceived as good, Jesus calls evil.

We must understand what it is that Jesus is saying here, because our lives depend on it, both now and forever. The Greek word for "evildoers" is rendered in various ways. The King James Version is painfully descriptive: "ye that work iniquity." A few translations are more literal: "you who practice lawlessness" (NKJV) and "you lawbreakers!" (NET). All are correct, but none by itself can capture the full meaning. The Greek word (*anomia*) literally means "no law" or "against the law" and was used to describe either wrongdoing in general or a sinful act. Jesus' use of the term in 7:23 must be seen in the context of his Sermon, in which his focus is on God's righteousness coming alive in the kingdom of the heavens. In Matthew 23 Jesus fills out the definition of *anomia* as he raises a succession of woes against the scribes and Pharisees who do not practice what they preach: they do things to be seen by others, they keep people out of the kingdom of the heavens, they swear falsely, they neglect others, and they are greedy and self-indulgent. Then, before he concludes with a scathing woe that implicates them in the killing of innocent prophets, Jesus exclaims, "Woe to you, scribes and Pharisees, hypocrites! For you are like whitewashed tombs, which on the outside look beautiful, but inside they are full of the bones of the dead and of all kinds of filth. So you also on the outside look righteous to others, but inside you are full of hypocrisy and lawlessness" (Matthew 23:27-28).

Jesus compares the false appearance of righteousness on the outside with the inner condition of lawlessness (*anomia*). That parallels his response to the self-righteous who will call him "Lord, Lord" (7:23). They have more interest in doing what they think looks good than in doing the will of the Father in the heavens.

In Jesus' sight, the lawbreakers he addresses in 7:23 have done something good that is bad! What might have been done in God's goodness was done for the wrong reason, and that is not acceptable in God's book. Persons in poverty may be helped by groceries received from an arrogant person who wants to appear good, but that arrogant person is not acting from within the law of God's righteousness. A local church may implement educational ministries for the neighborhood but may do so to promote themselves. Jesus said, "Give alms in secret, pray in secret, and fast in secret, for that is how your Father sees things." Isn't it ironic that those who try so hard to achieve righteousness by fulfilling the letter of the law are the ones Jesus calls lawbreakers? God's righteousness is found beyond the law, and it is only those who excel in that pursuit who enter the kingdom of the heavens (see Matthew 5:20).

To conclude his momentous and unsurpassed sermon, Jesus tells the parable of the wise and foolish builders in 7:24-27. The rock of righteousness is a firm foundation, but the sand of unrighteousness is precarious and unreliable. To build on the words Jesus has delivered is to do righteousness. *Not* to build on his words is to do unrighteousness. Whatever is built on the rock will stand, and whatever is built on the sand will perish—its fall will be great! Jesus says that everyone who hears his words and acts on them (Greek: *does* them) will be like someone wise. In eternal contrast, everyone who hears his words and does not act on them (Greek: *does* them *not*) will be like someone foolish.

In its unpretentious way, the little verb "to do" makes a big impact. Translators use various English words to interpret the Greek word for "to do" (*poiein*), and rightly so. But differing translations can hide relationships that develop between passages of Scripture. Throughout the Sermon on the Mount, important concepts have taken shape based on doing and not doing, according to that little Greek word. For example, in Matthew 5:19 Jesus says that anyone who breaks even the least of the law's commands and teaches that same disobedience to others will be called least in the kingdom of the heavens, but anyone who *does* them and teaches that same obedience to others will be called great in the kingdom of the heavens. In 6:1 Jesus tells his listeners "not to *do* your righteousness" before others to be seen by them. The golden rule tells us to *do* to others as we would have them *do* to us (see 7:12). And in 7:17-19 Jesus tells about the good and bad trees that bear fruit, each according to their particular character. You guessed it—the word for "bear" in the Greek is the same little word *do*. The good tree "does" good fruit and the bad tree "does" bad fruit. A good tree cannot "do" bad fruit, nor can a bad tree "do" good fruit. And every tree not "doing" good fruit is destroyed. So when Jesus says that everyone who hears his words and *does them* will be like someone wise, we exclaim, "Yes, I understand!" And when he says that everyone who hears his words and *does them not*, we admit self-consciously, "I understand that too." One day,

> as Jesus was speaking to the crowd, his mother and brothers were outside, wanting to talk with him. Someone told Jesus, "Your mother and your brothers are outside, and they want to speak to you." Jesus asked, "Who is my mother? Who are my brothers?" Then he pointed to his disciples and said, "These are my mother and brothers. *Anyone who does the will of my Father in [the heavens]* is my brother and sister and mother!" (Matthew 12:46-50 NLT, italics added).

The apostle James charges Christians to be "doers of the word, and not hearers only" (James 1:22 KJV) and comments on the seemingly endless argument of faith versus works (2:14-26). The Greek word for our word *faith* is rich in meaning and can be translated as both *faith* and *faithfulness*. James says that faith without works is dead (2:17). If we use the word *faithfulness*, the former discussion becomes meaningless. "Faithfulness without works is dead" states an impossibility, since *faithfulness* means "living out one's faith." There is no faith without faithfulness, and no faithfulness without works. If we wisely *do* what Jesus teaches, we are faithful. If we foolishly *do not do* what Jesus teaches, we are unfaithful. The apostle Paul picks up on that contrast and compares it to doing the will of the Father in the heavens: "Be very careful, then, how you live—not as unwise but as wise, making the most of every opportunity, because the days are evil. Therefore do not be foolish, but understand what the Lord's will is" (Ephesians 5:15-17 TNIV).

Either we are faithful to God or we are not. Either we do righteousness or we do not. Doing the will of God is sometimes loud and energetic, sometimes quiet and reflective. It's not the doing of deeds, but the doing of God's will. It's not fulfilling our own desires, but seeking the face of God. Those "many" who will come to Jesus saying, "Lord, Lord," will ask him as proof of their seeming righteous character, "Did we not *do* many deeds of power in your name?" But Jesus will answer, "I never knew you. Go away from me, you lawbreakers!" (Matthew 7:23 NET).

As Jesus comes to the close of his amazing sermon, we know it is not only the crowds who are astounded (7:28-29) but ourselves, as well. Jesus has shown that God's righteousness is available to followers of Christ. But more than that, God wants to shower on them all the blessings of the kingdom of the heavens. Those blessings are the good gifts that come from the Father in the heavens, even greater than the best gifts parents can imagine for their children. Those who seek the righteousness of the kingdom have everything they need. Mutual love and forgiveness will show up in the spiritual, material, and social areas of everyday life. And on the day of the Lord, those who already have begun to live that kingdom on earth will enjoy the full, magnificent bounty of the kingdom of the heavens. With thankful surprise we realize it is through ordinary people, through us, through the amazing community of heaven on earth that God's blessings of grace, joy, and peace can flow out to the whole world. That's the righteousness of God.

For Discussion

We hear statements like, "She sure is a good Christian" or "I hired him because he's a good Christian." What makes a good Christian? If there are good Christians, by definition there must also be bad Christians. Is that possible? What adjectives might be used to describe "Christian"? Certainly *new* or *longtime* would be appropriate. Anything else? What does it mean to be Christian?

Frank has been attending Sunday worship and participating in midweek Bible study regularly. He enthusiastically shares his Christian testimony in various settings. Occasionally you find him helping at the city soup kitchen or assisting at the local boys club. Frank also has a shaved head, a full red beard, an earring, some colorful tattoos, a black leather jacket, and a Harley. He has been known to drink a beer or two. Now he is seeking official membership in your rather traditional congregation. What happens next?

A noteworthy reminder from author Albert H. Epp: "Unfortunately, often Christians have a vision so small, they need no divine help to fulfill it!"[2] How does that relate to the ministry of your congregation?

Call to Commitment
Beyond the Sacred Page

> *Beyond the sacred page*
> *I seek thee, Lord;*
> *my spirit pants for thee,*
> *O living Word.*
> —Mary A. Lathbury, 1877[1]

Well over a century ago, Mary A. Lathbury had it right. There is no word of law here, no set of rules, no rigid formula. Only earnest longing to move beyond human limitation to find the living Word. Only deep thirsting to enter the presence of the righteous one, who reigns beyond the law, beyond the sacred page.

Composer Alice Parker asserted, "The written page represents only 5 to 10 percent of the music. The page is a necessary evil, but it is an evil."[2] But for some performers, the evil page has become sacred: they think music happens simply by reproducing the pitches and rhythmic patterns printed on the page. Not possible, says Parker. "Written music is a contradiction in terms: a visual graph of an audible phenomenon. It is by nature incomplete, imprecise and simplistic. But it is what we've got, and if you realize these shortcomings, you can work with it."[3]

Parker's words ring true. My composer son, Jim, and I spent a pleasant and remarkable time at one of her fellowships for teachers, performers, and composers. Along with a handful of other musicians, we sang and composed and listened. Drawing on experience and wisdom gained from a lifetime in music, Parker ushered us into the realm of music beyond the page.

There in the beautiful Berkshire Hills of western Massachusetts, invigorated by her teaching and surrounded by the inviting atmosphere of her studio, it dawned on me that her view of the printed page was the same as Lathbury's. When performers see the printed page as sacred, it becomes law. By obeying the rules of the musical score, they assume they can produce music, but they are limiting themselves to a meager representation of the real thing. If the page says to play or sing a phrase smoothly and softly, pharisaical performers make every effort to obey those directions along with any other notes, marks, and written instructions. But that's the extent of it, and the performance turns into an empty display of technical prowess that shows only how well the "sacred page" has been reproduced.

In contrast, musicians who go beyond the particulars of the score become instruments who reveal the music that inspired the printed page in the first place. They sing and play with a grace and beauty that connects with listeners because genuine music is being heard. For authentic performers, the printed page only confirms and guides what they already have begun to know about the music that lies beyond the score. They have moved beyond the sacred page to get in touch with the music itself.

To make their music available to performers, composers are constrained to work within the fixed parameters of the written page because, as Parker says, "It is what we've got." Notes on lines and spaces, familiar rhythmic patterns, and unique markings and directions give composers a limited means by which to sketch an outline of what needs to happen so their music can sound. But there are not enough notes, markings, and written directions available to capture music itself, so performers are needed to fill out those markings so music can happen. At all times, faithful performers—soloists, ensembles, worshipping congregations—must find appropriate ways to let music itself come to life in whatever physical, emotional, and spiritual settings it is used. The printed score provides only one doorway into the music; it can never replace the music. The late Victor Borge, musician, pianist, and comedian, asked a person sitting in the front row if she liked piano music. To her affirmative nod, Borge responded, "Here's some," and handed her a score. We laugh because we catch the difference between the page and the music. It takes performers to reveal what lies beyond the page.

God is composer. But because the music of God's righteousness comes from beyond everyday human understanding, God sent Jesus in human flesh to embody that music among us. God had acted among the people of Israel and had given the written law, but that was not enough. Jesus came as the genuine music of God's goodness "and dwelt among us, and we beheld His glory, the glory as of the only begotten of the Father, full of grace and truth" (John 1:14 NKJV). When Jesus returned to heaven, God sent the Holy Spirit to the members of the kingdom of the heavens to reveal the glory of God. That is the divine plan, but we as "performers" sometimes find ourselves caught in trying to pronounce and distribute God's righteousness by obeying the notes of the sacred page, rather than by finding and knowing the music that inspired it. We may even make the form of our obedience a sacred object, whether it be our denomination, our style of worship, or our theology of the end times. When that happens, righteousness becomes a specific item or act—an idol. It's dead. It's not the real thing. Righteousness comes only in the process that invites the goodness of God to flow through us and shower its blessings on others. I finally came to understand that I wasn't playing the piano, but was playing music by means of the piano. With Lathbury, it is essential to go beyond the sacred page to seek the Lord, the *living* Word.

Jesus responded to those who challenged his identity as God's Son, and he spoke clearly of his relationship to the sacred page: "You have your heads in your Bibles constantly because you think you'll find eternal life there. But you miss the forest for the trees. These Scriptures are all about me! And here I am, standing right before you, and you aren't willing to receive from me the life you say you want" (John 5:39-40 Msg).

I must confess, regretfully, to too much of my own rules-oriented "unperformance" of the sacred page, both in music and in my Christian life. But I also testify to the joy and satisfaction of performing from within the bounteous 90 to 95 percent of the music that lies beyond the page. To know such intimate communion with the original music is beyond description. It is gift. To dutifully perform only the law of the page does not hold a candle to the true light that shines beyond it.

Too much music never gets heard because the rules get in the way—"You have your heads in your Bibles." When we perform a piece of music, Parker says we need to be aware of countless things beyond the score: its ethnic origins and local customs, what kind of dance it is, whether it is a love song or lullaby, whether it was created for instruments or voices, when it was composed or improvised or first sung.[4] When we perform the music of God's righteousness, Jesus says we need to

> abide in me as I abide in you. Just as the branch cannot bear fruit by itself unless it abides in the vine, neither can you unless you abide in me. I am the vine, you are the branches. Those who abide in me and I in them bear much fruit, because apart from me you can do nothing. (John 15:4-5)

To abide in Christ means to remain in him, stay in him. It means to live in him. It means to give complete loyalty to Christ. I ask myself how I fare in living out my faithfulness to him in the spiritual, material, and social areas of everyday life.

Can I honestly declare my loyalty to Jesus and then follow through on that? If not, what gets in the way? Do other loyalties take precedence? The writer of 1 John says, "If you love the world, love for the Father is not in you" (2:15 TNIV).

As individual Christians and as the entire kingdom of the heavens, we are called to commit ourselves to the mission of God in Christ. What form would that take if our commitment were more than just following rules? How might we go beyond the law to seek the living Word? How might we live out God's righteousness? Rebekah, a young friend of mine, says that a horse can swim, but it is designed to run. I can't help but think that the church is swimming but is designed to run, that we are seeing only a small portion of the potential entrusted to us by God. Christianity is not our attempt to be good or a way to control those around us. It is not a code of law or a set of slogans to be hurled at the world. Christianity is God's goodness lavished on the world through Jesus Christ, and it takes shape in the everyday life of the church. Blest is the church, for theirs is the kingdom of the heavens!

If we desire that God's Spirit transform our whole life, it is not possible to reserve some parts of our daily routine for inside the kingdom of the heavens and some for outside. To live beyond the law pertains to everything we do, and certainly to more than regularly going to church on Sunday morning, making financial contributions to charities, and driving the speed limit—although God's righteousness would include them. And what about relating to neighbors, fulfilling expectations at work, raising children, and filling out tax returns? What about congregations and denominations accepting each other, cooperating in local and national projects, and recognizing each other as brothers and sisters in Christ? Since 1729, when satirist Jonathan Swift wrote *A Modest Proposal* for dealing with the poor children of Ireland, innumerable "modest proposals" have been made. You may remember this one for peace: "Let the Christians of the world agree that they will not kill each other." Which raises a significant question: Why would Christians kill anyone? What is it that gets in the way of our living as Christ taught? Where do we place our first loyalty as Christians?

We balk at the seemingly hard saying of Jesus to love our enemies. Isn't there some Greek word to show that Jesus didn't really mean that? No. God's children are those who truly reflect the character of God's family, and in that way they are perfect as the heavenly Father is perfect. In 1967 sociologist Stanley Milgram proposed the proverbial "six degrees of separation," which maintains that each person is separated from any other on the planet by a chain of acquaintances with no more than five people between them. That idea was confirmed in recent years when researchers at Columbia University conducted a modern version of Milgram's study on the Internet.[5] So if you and I and all our friends each loved six neighbors of ours, and all of those persons loved six neighbors of theirs, and so on, all of us would be loving people we know, and there would be no enemies to be loved—around the world! Crazy? Maybe, maybe not. Perhaps it's really the loving of neighbors that's tough.

All of that gets my mind whirling, and I've come up with a few modest proposals of my own. What if Christians of the world—or just in our neighborhoods—agreed they would not speak ill of each other, would not sue each other, would not get impatient with each other in traffic, would not treat each other's children rudely, would not butt into line ahead of each other? From another perspective, what if all Christians blessed each other by speaking well of each other, by assisting each other with legal matters, by being courteous with each other in traffic, by welcoming each other's children in their home, by making sure that others are served ahead of them? It sounds like instructions for an elementary school class. Embarrassing, isn't it? When I reflect on how I sometimes act, I probably should not tell others that I'm a Christian, like that young man who does not put Christian bumper stickers on his car. Maybe it's easier for me to display the Ten Commandments in order to tell others how they should live than to live the Beatitudes in order to let others know how the kingdom of the heavens intends to bless them—through me.

A small group of Christian men has met one night every two weeks over a number of years. They do so to relate to each other for accountability. They don't have rules, but they have questions to ask and to answer every time they meet. It is a way of Christian life, a commitment they have made to follow Jesus, not a code of law. This is what they ask each other when they get together:

1. Have you been with anyone anywhere that would appear as compromising?
2. Have you entertained any inappropriate fantasies in your thought life?
3. Have you viewed or read any sexually explicit material?
4. Have any of your financial dealings lacked integrity?
5. Have you spent adequate time in Bible study and prayer?
6. Have you given priority to your family?
7. Have you been faithful to your commission of Christian service?
8. Have you just lied to me?

What if Christian congregations were just as intentional and clear, not by creating lists of what members should do, but by developing opportunities for being open with each other? Groups could plan their own system of accountability. We could openly confess and forgive, and we could explore how God is working among us. I think of small congregations of ordinary people. But I also think of public figures and leaders of our large churches and of government. When and where do they sit down brother to brother and sister to sister, opening themselves before each other to receive God's word among them?

How can we express our loyalty and faithfulness to God? For citizens of the United States, pledging allegiance to the flag has been on the front burner, especially since June 2002. What would it mean if Christians in the United States and around the world were to pledge allegiance to the Lord, the living Word? Is that possible? The experience of J. Nelson Kraybill, president of Associated Mennonite Biblical Seminary in Elkhart, Indiana, confirms the sensitivity and strong commitment it could take. In a 1999 article on the book of Revelation, he told how important it is for Christians in every country to think through how and why they engage in expressions of political loyalty, and illustrated his point with this personal story:

> Not long after I moved back to the United States after six years in England, I attended a meeting of a local civic club in Indiana. There was prayer before the meal, after which the club members repeated a promise of commitment to honesty, international understanding, and fair business practice. Finally, everyone pledged allegiance to the U.S. flag.
>
> Having been raised in a Mennonite community where we did not show that kind of loyalty to a nation—although we respected and prayed for it—I have never saluted the flag or said the pledge. So I stood quietly and thanked God for all that is right and good about this country. I prayed this powerful nation would use its enormous resources for the good of all humanity, not just for Americans.
>
> When the meal started, a friendly voice at the table said, "So, you're English?" No, I answered. "Oh, you must be Canadian." Then I realized that others had noticed I did not say the pledge of allegiance. "I love this country," I started, "and I'm grateful for opportunities and freedoms I have here. But I am first of all a Christian, and I have Christian brothers and sisters around the world. My citizenship is with anyone who follows Jesus, and it's hard for me to pledge allegiance to anything else."[6]

Five years later, now with the added perspective of the aftermath to 9/11 and the 2002 ruling on the pledge of allegiance, Kraybill and seminary professor June Alliman Yoder drafted a Christian pledge. It focuses on "loyalty to a Trinitarian God known most fully in Jesus Christ [and] highlights the fact that our highest allegiance is to a global people of God, not to a territorial political entity."

> I pledge allegiance to Jesus Christ,
> And to God's kingdom for which he died—
> One Spirit-led people the world over, indivisible,
> With love and justice for all.[7]

What is my sacred page? When do I consider that my head may be stuck in the pages of the Bible and I'm missing Jesus standing right in front of me? Where is the point at which I must decide it's either my will or God's? Can the church be satisfied only to swim when it has the thrilling capacity to run? How can the church become the authentic instrument of God's goodness in order to perform the music of God's righteousness? A group of fifteen scholars met periodically from 1998 to 2002 at the Center of Theological Inquiry in Princeton, New Jersey, to engage in The Scripture Project. One of the nine theses they settled on said,

> Scripture is like a musical score that must be played or sung in order to be understood; therefore, the church interprets scripture by forming communities of prayer, service, and faithful witness. The Psalms, for example, are "scores" awaiting performance by the community of faith. They school us in prayer and form in us the capacities for praise, penitence, reflection, patient endurance and resistance to evil.[8]

Mary A. Lathbury and Alice Parker speak the same language, sing the same song. The church of Jesus Christ is designed to go beyond the sacred page to seek the Lord, to pant for the living Word. The Christian church interprets the righteousness of God in its spiritual, material, and social areas of everyday life, and in so doing, proclaims the gospel of Christ. The kingdom of the heavens is the incarnation of God on earth.

When Zerubbabel was sent to rebuild the temple in Jerusalem, the word of the Lord came through the prophet: "Not by might, nor by power, but by my spirit, says the LORD of hosts" (Zechariah 4:6). It is the same for God's church today. Law and rules exist through human might and power. Suppose we substituted the words *law* and *rules* for *might* and *power*—"Not by law, nor by rules, but by my spirit, says the LORD of hosts." God's Spirit, promised by Jesus and sent to teach and guide the church, is beyond human imagination and strength. The apostle Paul says that the kingdom of the heavens has not received the spirit of the kingdoms of the world, but the Spirit from God (see 1 Corinthians 2:12). The law written in ink kills, but the Spirit brings life and freedom (see 2 Corinthians 3:6, 17). If you walk by the Spirit "you will not gratify the desires of the sinful nature. . . . [And] if you are led by the Spirit, you are not under the law" (Galatians 5:16, 18 TNIV). Paul repeats what Jesus had said: our righteousness must go beyond that of the scribes and Pharisees in order for us to enter the kingdom of the heavens.

What Jesus embodied in his earthly life, the Sermon on the Mount tells us in words. Jesus invites us to come beyond his words to meet and to know the eternal presence of God, the inspiration and source of Christ's own love and sacrifice. If we don't go beyond the limitations of righteousness as contained in laws, rules, and sacred pages, we never will enter the kingdom of the heavens. "Seek that kingdom as your first priority," Jesus says, "and all the things you need will be available to you. Apply kingdom attributes to your daily life at home, in your community, in your country, and around the world. Get to know me so that I know you, and the will of our Father in the heavens will be accomplished" (PKC). Theologian and scholar Clarence Bauman sums it up in his book on the Sermon.

It is not enough to preserve the sayings of Jesus in their original purity in order to hand them down unaltered from generation to generation like mandatory yoga exercises for spiritual formation. Truth is not a static possession but a dynamic inspiration. To truly hear the Sermon on the Mount is to be inspired by the spirit and will of Jesus to venture our own way illumined by its light.[9]

Sally Morganthaler, a Lutheran expert on postmodern trends, says that people are tired of rules, regulations, and words about what you have to do to get to God. She says, "In a postmodern world, encounter trumps argument every time. Most of all, postmodern people want an encounter with God through us [which means that as Christians] we get beyond the mind of God to the person of God, the heart of God, the spirit of God."[10]

When the Lord of righteousness offers us the kingdom of the heavens, why should we shape our own kingdom with finite limitations? How long should we resist God's desire to create within us the freedom of the living Word, to make us into the loving, attractive community intended for us all along? As the *koinonia* of Christ—the fellowship of those who have been called into the kingdom of the heavens as partners with Christ—we have been given the secrets of the kingdom of the heavens (see Matthew 13:11). Let us as Christ's community gratefully and joyfully receive the blessing of God that comes to everyone in the kingdom: the poor in spirit, those who mourn, the meek, those who hunger for righteousness, the merciful, the pure in heart, the peacemakers, those who are persecuted, or whatever our lot. Let us make God's rich blessings available to everyone. Let us be transformed by the power that flows to us from the throne of God through the Holy Spirit, so that God-Among-Us-And-Within-Us can guide us and teach us and mold us into the full stature of Christ. And may those who encounter such a beau-

tiful body be overwhelmed by the goodness of God's righteousness and be drawn into the loving center of its amazing,
generous life.

Our Father, the One in the heavens,
Holy, Infinite Presence
beyond all human understanding.
Your kingdom come,
Your will be done,
here on earth as it is in heaven.
Give us today our daily bread.
And forgive us our sins,
as we also forgive those who sin against us.
And do not let us face more than we can bear,
but rescue us from the evil one.
　　　　　　　—Matthew 6:9-13 (PKC)

Then I heard every creature
in heaven and on earth
and under the earth and in the sea,
and all that is in them, singing,
"To the one seated on the throne and to the Lamb
be blessing and honor and glory and might
forever and ever!"
　　　　　　　—Revelation 5:13

AMEN!

For Discussion

Your fellowship of Christian believers is located near an area of needy people, many of whom do not speak English and a number of whom may be illegal immigrants. What does your fellowship do?

There is no Christian nation. So, what happens when the expectations of the kingdom of God come into conflict with the expectations of the kingdom of your country? How do you honor your country's flag and the kingdom of Christ when they don't agree? In the United States, the pledge of allegiance to the flag includes "one nation, under God." It is one thing to pledge it, but another to live it. Which flag is on top and which is "under" the other? Who discerns and speaks God's word—government officials, church leaders, the Holy Spirit in community?

Mark Twain has been quoted as saying something like, "It ain't the parts of the Bible I don't understand that bother me, it's the parts that I do understand." It appears obvious that no one fully understands the full Bible. And even if we did, that is not enough. With Twain, we might confess our sometimes less than sterling commitment to what we already know of Jesus Christ, the living Word. How do you plan to go "beyond the sacred page"?

Conclusion
A Personal Letter

My dear sister,

When you came to me that Sunday morning and asked, "What does your church allow?" I didn't give you a good answer. My tongue was tied because I didn't know where to begin. I knew that there would be too much to handle in a brief conversation. "Church" involves so many good things and is so wonderful that a question about it is always important. But when you asked your question about our congregation, I knew I couldn't deal adequately with it, so I mumbled some kind of stock answer, hoping it would be sufficient until later. I hope I at least sounded welcoming.

My predicament may seem strange to you, but let me explain. My difficulty in answering your question was not because it was you who asked it or because it was wrong to ask it or because what you asked was off limits. You had, and still have, every right to a good answer, one that fully satisfies your question. Every person who inquires about church, including those outside the church, should receive a good answer. My difficulty is that I hear and see the same question among church members all the time: "What does church allow?" People seem to get stuck at that point, but I wish they would grow beyond it. When you spoke with me, I believe you were innocently putting into words what you had candidly observed about church in general, and that is what troubles me. To say that the church "allows" something brings forward all kinds of assumptions and considerations. Let me explain what I mean, and then I may be able to answer your question.

A passage in the New Testament letter to the Hebrews expresses my feelings. In chapter 5 the writer, whoever it was, is disappointed that those who were to receive the letter needed to be retaught the basics of Christianity. By this time they should have grown off milk for babies and on to solid food for adults; they should be teaching others, rather than needing to be taught. That's the same today. It is necessary for infants in the faith to drink the milk of God's love and acceptance, but it is just as necessary for those who are growing up in the faith to be feasting on the solid food that is God's righteousness. The writer says that "infants" are unacquainted with the word of righteousness but that "mature ones" have learned to distinguish both good and evil. To me, that gets to the heart of what it means to be the fellowship we call church. Knowing good from evil is a gift from God that brings freedom to those who follow Jesus. To know right from wrong without having a checklist of do's and don'ts is a mark of Christian maturity.

Jesus told those who wanted to follow him that he wouldn't look so much at *what* they did but at *why* they did it and *how* they did it. He called it "doing the will of the Father in the heavens." He said a congregation that does the will of God is like a tree that is good all the way from the tips of its roots to the tips of its branches. A good tree like that can't help but produce good fruit. In contrast, people who try to do good things to make themselves good are like bad trees that produce bad fruit. You see, it's not the fruit that makes the tree—it's the tree that makes the fruit. Good trees are planted and tended by the goodness of God. The writer of Hebrews says that those who have not yet learned good from evil are still infants because they have not yet developed a sense of God's righteousness.

Righteousness, we may think, is some unapproachable church topic for intellectuals to discuss, so we tie it up in a bundle and throw it into a big theological bin, out of sight. Even if we do grasp some of its meaning, we may think righteousness can be achieved only by those who appear to be especially good or holy and who know all the right words—and that leaves us out. But I am so happy to tell you that's all wrong! Righteousness is the gracious character of God that fills the body of Christian believers so full that all of God's goodness cannot be contained within them; it overflows from the lives of those ordinary, loving people and rains down as showers of blessing on everyone they touch. Righteousness is the beautiful, day-to-day expression of God's goodness on earth as it comes to life in people like you and me. Jesus himself became a human being like us, precisely to show everyone what God is like. And now Jesus has passed on that awesome and joyful responsibility to all who know him as "Lord."

Jesus wants the Christian church to be God "in the flesh," just as he was, to show people what God is like. We do that by allowing God's Spirit to make us into "good trees," not by doing good things. Anyone can obey a traffic light or pay taxes on time. Anyone can go to church on Sunday and pray out loud and give huge offerings of money. But that doesn't make them holy or even special—maybe just proud of what they've done. Jesus said that to be members of his church we must follow him, not church laws. The whole church as a body must follow Jesus. In the familiar Lord's Prayer, Jesus taught the Christian community to pray that heaven would come to earth among us, so that through our "heavenly community" God's will would be done on earth. In such a community, Jesus said, people depend on each other and forgive each other. Together they embody God in their everyday life.

So when you ask, "What does your church allow?" you see that I can't just hand you a list of regulations. Church isn't that way. It is dynamic and loving, and it vibrantly responds to whatever faces it from day to day. The church is a fellowship of Christ that welcomes the voice of God among its members through the presence of the Holy Spirit. In that way, the church really doesn't "allow" anything in terms of a code of law. But, come to think of it, the church does allow one thing: it allows God's righteousness to flow through its body to everyone around!

Since the time you spoke with me, the church I called "our congregation" has faithfully committed itself to understanding how God lives and moves among ordinary people. For some years now, they have earnestly examined themselves in light of the Scriptures, with the intent of becoming who God wants them to be. In ways they did not know previously, they have begun to see that they are a congregation of God's people made alive through Christ and guided by the Holy Spirit. "Church," they've discovered, is not a bunch of individuals doing their own good things but a fellowship in which every member brings unique gifts to be used in the ministry of Christ. And everyone is part of that ministry, from youngest to oldest.

That's not always easy to do, because it is clear to everyone that each person is a human being and therefore open to sin's temptations. But that's what is so great about being a member of the "heavenly community." Jesus promised that whenever people seek to be part of it and make it their first priority, God's righteousness shows up there, blessing and reshaping the community according to divine purpose. If compassion is needed, it's there. If forgiveness is needed, it's there. If reconciliation is needed, it's there. All the riches of God's blessings are lavished on that community for their own good and for the good of everyone they reach.

I'm so glad you asked your question! You can see that it kept nudging me until I found a suitable answer. And in the process, my own spiritual understandings have grown. But I am sorry that it took me so long to get in touch with you. With my letter, I'm including a copy of the congregation's mission statement, which they put together after you left. If they already had made such a declaration of purpose and identity when you first had come to me, I really wonder if you would have needed to ask your question. I hope not. Anyway, here it is.

I pray that you—and the church around the world—will allow yourself to dance and sing in the beautiful righteousness of God.

Your friend, and one minister among many,

Mission Statement of
Beaverdam Mennonite Church,
Corry, Pennsylvania

HONESTLY ADMITTING
our need of forgiveness

THANKFULLY PROCLAIMING
that God rescues us

FAITHFULLY BEING
the eyes, ears, mouth,
hands and feet of Jesus

JOYFULLY LIVING
by the power of the Holy Spirit

For Discussion

In your congregation, what does membership mean?

How do people of your congregation relate to each other—as family, friends, co-workers, followers of a leader? Where does the power lie? Who are the leaders and why? How would you describe the community of your congregation?

How do people come into your congregation according to the three Bs: believing, behaving, belonging? By first *believing* to know how to *behave* so they can *belong*? By *belonging*, which leads to *believing*, which results in *behaving*? Do they *behave* first, so they can *belong* in order to *believe*? Is there a best order?

Appendix 1
Structure of the Sermon on the Mount

The Sermon on the Mount takes its title from the words in Matthew 5:1, "When Jesus saw the crowds, he went up the mountain." It can be debated whether or not Jesus literally preached Matthew 5, 6, and 7 as a single sermon to people gathered on a mountainside. He certainly could have done that, but Matthew's written version could also be a compilation based on parts of individual sermons that Jesus preached on numerous occasions, varying the length and content in order to address his immediate listeners. Such a practice is not unlike that of today's public speakers, preachers, and evangelists as they address varying constituencies. No matter the exact setting, Matthew has carefully constructed the discourse to reveal Jesus' divine plan for shaping a community according to God's purpose and will.

Today the many available versions of the Bible include outlines, headings, and footnotes, along with study notes. But the original configuration and language of the New Testament did not include such plentiful directions. There were no chapter divisions or numbered verses. The normal punctuation and quotation marks we've come to expect were not there. So Bible translators and scholars take nothing for granted; they look for clues in each specific passage and its context as they prepare the treasure of the Scripture for us. Consequently, we find numerous interpretations and explanations of certain Bible passages, which surely is the case with our subject at hand. As I too look closely at the Sermon on the Mount, I am building on a foundation that many before me have laid. The following diagram shows my understanding of how the Sermon develops and how its parts relate to each other.

Sermon on the Mount
Matthew 5–7

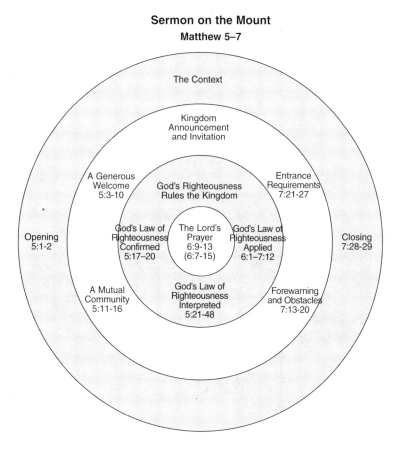

The Context

Kingdom
Announcement
and Invitation

A Generous
Welcome
5:3-10

God's Righteousness
Rules the Kingdom

Entrance
Requirements
7:21-27

Opening
5:1-2

God's Law of
Righteousness
Confirmed
5:17–20

The Lord's
Prayer
6:9-13
(6:7-15)

God's Law of
Righteousness
Applied
6:1–7:12

Closing
7:28-29

A Mutual
Community
5:11-16

God's Law of
Righteousness
Interpreted
5:21-48

Forewarning
and Obstacles
7:13-20

At the very center stands the Lord's Prayer, which proclaims the character of God's kingdom. Everything in the circle relates to the Lord's Prayer, emanating from it, pointing to it, and in some way pertaining to it. The material that surrounds that seminal prayer is Jesus' monumental teaching on God's law of righteousness—its validity, its nature, its practicality. The next surrounding layer includes the announcement of the kingdom with which Jesus starts the Sermon, as well as the invitation to the kingdom with which he closes it. His announcement tells who is welcomed by the kingdom of the heavens and how it is organized. His invitation warns of possible ambushes and hurdles, and tells how to gain entry. Surrounding the entire sermon is the context of Jesus' ministry to the crowds. Although each layer has its own purpose, all parts relate to every other part within the full circle, and together everything in the Sermon is a proclamation of the good news of God's righteous kingdom.

The following outline provides a sequential view of the parts.

Sermon on the Mount, Matthew 5:1—7:29

1. Opening (5:1-2)
The sermon discourse connects to the preceding narrative (4:23-25) and identifies the crowds and disciples as listeners.

2. Jesus Announces the Kingdom of the Heavens (5:3-16)
    a. A Generous Welcome (5:3-10)
Persons with various types of characteristics and needs are listed to illustrate the innumerable variety of people welcomed by the kingdom of the heavens.
    b. A Mutual Community (5:11-16)
The kingdom of the heavens is governed by those who fulfill God's righteousness, not by a hierarchical elite.

3. God's Righteousness Rules the Kingdom (5:17—7:12)
    a. God's Law of Righteousness Confirmed (5:17-20)
God's law of righteousness is forever true, but it must become
preeminent in the life of kingdom members.
    b. God's Law of Righteousness Interpreted (5:21-48)
Knowing the words of the law and faithfully living them are two
different things, as Jesus explains by using six examples with the
teaching device, "It was said, but I say."
    c. God's Law of Righteousness Applied (6:1—7:12)
Highlighting three major spheres of life, Jesus teaches how
members of the kingdom actually can live out God's law of
righteousness.
        i. The Spiritual Dimensions of Righteousness (6:1-18)
Proper doing of alms, prayer, and fasting provides the foundation of the spiritual life, and the Lord's Prayer, inserted here
(6:7-15), reveals the central core of meaning for the kingdom of
the heavens.
        ii. The Material Dimensions of Righteousness (6:19-34)
Members of the kingdom live within the goodness and security
of the kingdom, not trying to make a go of it in their own way
but depending on God, the source of all rightness.
        iii. The Social Dimensions of Righteousness (7:1-12)
Instead of setting themselves up as the standard by which to control others, kingdom members invite collaboration from others,
and good things of God come through the community.

4. Jesus Invites People into the Kingdom of the Heavens (7:13-27)
    a. Forewarning and Obstacles (7:13-20)
Jesus encourages his listeners to choose the path that leads to
life, being watchful of those who would lead them astray.
    b. Entrance Requirements (7:21-27)
Doing the will of the Father in the heavens is the one entrance
requirement, and it can be fulfilled by putting into practice the
law of God's righteousness.

5. Closing (7:28-29)
After hearing Jesus' teachings, the crowds are amazed at his
authority.

Appendix 2
Positions on Peace

Nowhere does the church of Christ stand out more in contrast from the state than when the state goes to war. Jesus told the Roman governor, Pilate, "My kingdom is not from this world. If my kingdom were from this world, my servants would be fighting to keep me from being handed over to the Jewish authorities. But as it is, my kingdom is not from here" (John 18:36 NET). Whenever the church chooses to fight, Jesus says, it is operating as a kingdom of the world, not as the kingdom of the heavens. War is the epitome of self-centered interest and controlling power. Jesus' message in the Sermon on the Mount, as elsewhere, introduces the kingdom of the heavens as the humble presence of God in the spiritual, material, and social spheres of everyday life. Wars are fought by kingdoms of this world, not by the kingdom of the heavens.

Jesus said there will be wars and rumors of wars (see Matthew 24:6), but he did not say that the church was to take part in them. The body of Christ carries out the ministry of reconciliation and makes disciples of all nations, baptizing them and teaching them to obey Christ's commands. That is the church for which Christ sacrificed himself. He wants the church to fulfill his mission of salvation, not fight for him. That's the good news, the gospel.

For the first several centuries after Christ's earthly sojourn, members of the Christian community largely refused to serve in the military. Although the precise reason is not known, it likely was because Jesus taught his followers to love their enemies and because the ruler of the Roman Empire claimed divinity—in contrast to the New Testament certainty that "Jesus Christ is Lord!" (Philippians 2:11).

In the early fourth century AD, the church was given legal status and protection under the Roman Emperor Constantine, a freedom it had not known previously. But in finding political freedom, the church began losing itself—a sad paradox. By 962 the relationship between church and state had become so closely connected that Pope John XII crowned Otto I as Roman emperor, inaugurating the Holy Roman Empire, which continued, in name at least, until 1806. But when church and state join to pursue the same agenda of aggression, even if for different reasons, the true identity of both kingdoms is lost. How can the church hear or speak God's prophetic word to the state when it sees God's purpose and the state's purpose as one?

Over the centuries, various groups of Christians have refused to engage in war and in so doing have run into trouble with the main body of the church, which has continued to align itself with the war-making authority of the state. How warfare is obedient to the word of God in Christ Jesus remains the big question. As followers of Jesus, how should the church relate to war? By using the example of World War II, in which Adolf Hitler and the Nazi regime were said to personify evil, a powerful argument is often made for the church's support of war. How could the church stand by and allow such wickedness? But it is not a question of whether there was cruelty, terror, or suffering. There was. The question is about how the church is to respond. States wage war, but the kingdom of the heavens does not.

I know a young man, a pastor now, who fought in the first Gulf War in 1991. He was not a Christian at that time, but because of his struggles with what had happened during the war, he sought out a Christian chaplain for help. Part of the chaplain's response was to admit that being a soldier is to involve yourself in an evil business. His challenge to the young man was to wrestle with the evil and try to find the good in what had been done.

The church needs to decide which kingdom it is in. When the church functions according to the law of God's righteousness, as Jesus taught in the Sermon on the Mount, it seeks first the kingdom of the heavens and its righteousness, and other needs are fulfilled as necessary. If the church cannot succeed in its mission by embodying the attributes of the kingdom of the heavens, we need to ask if it rightly has discerned its mission. Further, if it cannot achieve what it wants by living according to the kingdom of the heavens, should the church resort to the forceful means that other kingdoms use?

I like the question, "When is the best time to plant a tree?" The answer: "Twenty years ago." Those who argue for the church to involve itself in war say that love and respect don't stop nuclear missiles. But at what point do we raise that defense—now, or twenty years ago? There is always a long chain of cause and effect. What if the church faithfully embodied the attributes of Christ in our country's war against terror instead of so adamantly supporting the state's armed military attack? Not practical? Even though "nothing is impossible with God" (Luke 1:37)? Maybe we want to control the situation, rather than letting God do it. Whatever we do today does have a real effect on what will happen in the years to come, just as what was done years ago has shaped what is taking place today. The church must plant trees now! We can't go back, but we can act in the present.

In Nazi Germany the evangelical church supported the rise of Hitler. There the kingdom of the heavens aligned itself with the kingdom of the state and helped to make Hitler the leader he became. As a result, and as they've done in many wars, Christian brothers fought each other across the

European battlefields of World War II. How God mourns. If the church in Germany had refused to align itself with the state, what would have happened? We don't know; it's one of those "what ifs" that trouble the mind and heart. Possibly Hitler would not have become the tyrant he actually became, and World War II would not have happened. Just wishful thinking? Naive? Maybe. But it might be taking God's word seriously. What actions—or lack of them—during the years previous to World War II caused Hitler to think of the Jews as he did and caused the German Christians to respond to Hitler as they did?

When the catchphrase "What Would Jesus Do?" became popular nationally, numerous mutations hit the news. We were regaled with "What Would Jesus Drive?" and "What Would Jesus Eat?" and most of the variations were taken with a bit of humor. But one of them was not funny at all: "Who Would Jesus Bomb?" It sounds sacrilegious. Why? Because it is so contrary to what we know of Jesus. If we so easily can spot such a discrepancy with regard to Christ, how is it that we miss the incongruity when Christian people support their country's bombing of another? Might does not make right, especially if "right" is thought to be the same as "righteous."

God's law of righteousness comes as a humble child, not as a domineering adult, and it comes not by forcing the speck of sawdust from someone else's eye but by removing the log from our own. When a country is confronted by hostility and the churches in that country trade off the character of the kingdom of the heavens for the character of the kingdom of this world, the separation between church and state disappears. And they become one.

The main argument for the church to go to war along with the state appears to be the belief that Romans 13:1-7 commands it, or at least allows it. But the context of any Bible passage is always important for finding its meaning. When we examine the context of 13:1-7, we see that the apostle Paul in chapter 12 urges the Christian fellowship to claim its separateness from earthly kingdoms as the Christian way to fulfill God's purpose. (They were consecrated, sanctified, sacrificed! See 12:1.) The kingdom of the heavens, he says, does not follow the standards and practices of the world, but is transformed by following the will of God:

> Therefore I exhort you, brothers and sisters, by the mercies of God, to present your bodies as a sacrifice—alive, holy, and pleasing to God—which is your reasonable service. Do not be conformed to this present world, but be transformed by the renewing of your mind, so that you may test and approve what is the will of God—what is good and well-pleasing and perfect. (Romans 12:1-2 NET)

Paul teaches the gospel as Jesus taught it, that through God's mercies God's law of righteousness becomes manifest in those who do the will of the Father in the heavens: God's will is good and desirable and perfect! Those who live as God's children are perfect as the heavenly Father is perfect. In chapter 12 the apostle reminds the Christian community that each person bears the gifts of God for the good of all and that humility is the mark of God's generous love. The community should never take revenge on anyone, he says, because God takes care of that. In all of this, Paul says at the end, "Do not be overcome by evil, but overcome evil with good" (Romans 12:21). Don't fight evil with evil. The evil one may tempt you, and the kingdom of evil may try to penetrate the borders of your kingdom. But if God's people respond with evil, they themselves become evil, and evil has won out. Always respond with good. As Jesus said, you will recognize false prophets by their fruit. Good fruit comes from a good tree, and a good tree cannot bear evil fruit (see Matthew 7:15-20).

In Romans 13 the apostle says that because all governments are under God, the Christian community should be good citizens of the kingdom of the state. Many Christians interpret Paul's words as support for war, even in light of what he says in the previous chapter and in contrast to what Jesus teaches. Is Romans 13:1-7 an exception clause to the message of the whole New Testament? Is the kingdom of the heavens required to obey a kingdom of this world? Does the state dictate the law of God's righteousness? Does Romans 13 have different meanings, depending on where you live—Colombia, China, Pakistan, Iraq?

In his classic study, *The Politics of Jesus*, John Howard Yoder says that Romans 12 and 13 and the Sermon on the Mount speak the same language.[1] Both call for followers of Christ to be nonresistant in all relationships, including the social. Both call for disciples of Jesus to renounce the arrogance of dispensing what the world calls vengeance or justice. Both call Christians to respect and be subject to the kingdoms of the world, but not to understand the actions of those kingdoms as fulfilling the church's own reconciling ministry.

The Romans 13 text does not say that the kingdoms of the world are created, instituted, or ordained by God, only that God puts them in order. God does not declare any one government to be good or better than another. None of them is the church. Yoder writes, "Whatever government exists is ordered by God; but the text does not say that whatever the government does or asks of its citizens is good."[2] God's mercies, not the world's governments, are recognized as the foundation of the Christian community.

Yoder continues. The apostle tells the Christian community that God's way for them is not to return evil for evil or to avenge themselves (see 12:17, 19). In the same way, a government accomplishes its responsibilities only as it persistently "attends to the rewarding of good and evil according to their merits" (13:3-4). At the time Paul wrote, Rome was not engaged in major hostilities with any other nations. Yoder shows that the Roman function of "bearing the sword" represented the judicial and police function of the state and "in any orderly police system there are serious safeguards to keep the violence of the police from being applied in a wholesale way against the innocent."[3] Paul, says Yoder, was not telling the Roman Christians to *obey* the government but to subordinate themselves to it:

> Subordination is significantly different from obedience. The conscientious objector who refuses to do what his government asks him to do, but still remains under the sovereignty of that government and accepts the penalties which it imposes, or the Christian who refuses to worship Caesar but still permits Caesar to put him to death, is being subordinate even though he is not obeying.[4]

Paul's intent was to call the Christian Jews in Rome "away from any notion of revolution or insubordination. The call is to a nonresistant attitude toward a tyrannical government," as demonstrated by a life of suffering and serving love that speaks louder than aggressive rebellion.[5] When Christians subject themselves to their government, they follow the supreme example of Christ, who gave up heaven's riches to accept earthly subordination and humiliation (see Philippians 2:5-7).

In their impressive book, *Kingdom Ethics: Following Jesus in Contemporary Context*, Glen Stassen and David Gushee write that in the Sermon on the Mount

> Jesus was pointing in the direction of a culture of peacemaking rather than violence. . . . Jesus did not simply oppose evils such as killing, lying, and hating the enemy; *Jesus consistently emphasized a transforming initiative that could deliver us from the vicious cycle of violence or alienation.*[6]

Stassen and Gushee suggest a way out of that "vicious cycle" by committing significant thought to just war, nonviolence/pacifism and just peacemaking, and by identifying numerous resources on the subject of peace. In the mid-fourth century, Ambrose and Augustine introduced the idea of just war to show how the church might properly wage selected wars in God's name. Just war, Stassen and Gushee say, has found widespread acceptance from the fourth century to the present, at least in theory, but some believe it never has been put to use successfully, and others question whether it is even possible. Stassen and Gushee argue for more than only shallow adherence to the just war theory, because one must make a definite choice: the theory serves either "the purpose of reducing violence and seeking justice under Christ's lordship, or it serves some idolatrous loyalty such as rationalizing a war that we have an urge to make."[7] They hold that "any legitimate Christian use of just war theory must be based on nonviolence and justice, as taught by Jesus."[8]

The position of nonresistance, nonviolence, and Christian pacifism, say Stassen and Gushee, was adopted by various groups during the Middle Ages. Since the time of the Reformation, it has been claimed by the historic peace churches and by growing numbers of committed groups within the broader church. But there is considerable variation in how that position is perceived by those who embrace it, as well as by those who do not favor it. Some see it as inadequate to deal with the monstrous problem of war, not stopping to think that war works only half of the time or less (somebody always loses). Some see pacifism as doing nothing, which may be the stance of some pacifists but not of most. Others believe it is important not only to refrain from violence, but also to work for peace. To borrow wording from our discussion about the Sermon on the Mount, we could say that to be faithfully non-violent in Christ's image means to allow God's righteousness to flow through us, blessing all those around us, including the enemy. Extending that thought, Stassen and Gushee agree with what both Yoder and Dietrich Bonhoeffer so persuasively argued during the past century, and sum it up in their own words:

> Jesus really is Lord, and therefore the practices of peacemaking that Jesus taught for the church also have their normative relevance for the world. They are God's will. God is God over the whole world, not only over our private lives or only over the church. . . . This means that Christians, whether they are pacifists or just war theorists, are called to prod the government, and non-Christians, to adopt policies that are as nonviolent, as productive of nonviolence and as active in taking peacemaking initiatives, as possible. We cannot expect non-Christians to do this because of Christian faith; but because we believe the gospel reveals God's will, we must seek to persuade them to do peacemaking based on the ethics they do acknowledge.[9]

Whereas just war and nonviolence/pacifism deal mainly with the question of whether it is ever right to engage in war, Stassen and Gushee move on to propose what they believe must come first: just peacemaking. Just peacemaking is an attempt to prevent war and make peace. It is a positive theology of peacemaking. It is taking Jesus at his word. Advocates of just peacemaking believe that Jesus taught how to make peace, not just how to refrain from violence. Stassen and Gushee say just peacemaking is "based both on Jesus' way of peacemaking and on the obligation to do what is effective in preventing war." They give ten practices of just peacemaking that "can and do guide us in shaping the future that is God's will and our need."

1. *Support nonviolent direct action.* Revolutions around the world have been achieved through nonviolent direct action as practiced effectively by Mahatma Gandhi and Martin Luther King Jr.

2. *Take independent initiatives to reduce threat.* Initiatives that have been used to good effect include the strategy that freed Austria from Soviet domination in the 1950s, the

Atmospheric Test Ban Treaty of 1963, and the series of initiatives by Soviet President Gorbachev and the U.S. Congress to achieve dramatic reductions in nuclear weapons.

3. *Use cooperative conflict resolution.* Jesus taught in the Sermon on the Mount to make peace with anyone who may have something against you and then to worship (see Matthew 5:23-24). President Jimmy Carter's Camp David accords between Egypt and Israel, and his peaceful resolution of conflicts with Haiti and North Korea are examples. A key test of a government's claim to be seeking peace is whether it initiates negotiations or refuses them and whether it develops imaginative solutions that show it understands its adversary's perspectives and needs.

4. *Acknowledge responsibility for conflict and injustice; seek repentance and forgiveness.* A strong example is offered by the churches in Germany that confessed their sin of having supported Hitler and his unimaginable violence and injustice. Some other countries have followed with similar confessions for other actions.

5. *Promote democracy, human rights, and religious liberty.* "One implication of the effectiveness of democracy and human rights in preventing war is the obligation to spread democracy and human rights, including through laws limiting the dominance of money in elections. . . . Spreading peace is done by networks of persons willing to work together to gain public attention for protection against human rights violations."

6. *Foster just and sustainable economic development.* "A just peace requires an equitable world economy in which extreme inequalities in wealth, power, and participation are progressively overcome."

7. *Work with emerging cooperative forces in the international system.* The more nations are involved in a network of interaction, the less likely they are to engage in war. "Enemies" need to be invited into a constructive relationship of interaction.

8. *Strengthen the United Nations and other international organizations.* Such organizations "are resolving conflicts, monitoring, nurturing and even enforcing truces, and replacing violent conflict with the beginnings of cooperation." Alone, "states cannot solve problems of trade, debt and interest rates; of pollution, ozone depletion, acid rain, depletion of fish stocks and global warming; of migrations and refugees seeking asylum; of military security when weapons rapidly penetrate borders; and of international terrorism. The problems are international."

9. *Reduce offensive weapons and weapons trade.* For example, "Soviet President Gorbachev removed half the Soviet Union's tanks from Central Europe and all its river-crossing equipment, thus reducing the threat of a Soviet attack on Europe. This freed NATO to agree to get rid of all medium-range and shorter-range nuclear weapons from Western Europe—the first dramatic step in ending the Cold War peacefully."

10. *Encourage grassroots peacemaking groups and voluntary associations.* "Advocates of just peacemaking theory teach these effective practices, and their biblical grounding, in churches and other citizens' groups. And they test government actions, when governments claim to want peace, to see if they are taking these obligatory steps that do in fact lead to peace. They resist claims of politicians that we should vote for them because they claim to be Christian believers if they do not in fact do the things that make for peace, as Jesus taught." These groups "can help to initiate, foster and support transforming initiatives that take risks to break out of the cycles that perpetuate violence and injustice."[10]

I agree with Stassen and Gushee that just peacemaking will not prevent all wars, but it is a way to move into the arena of action instead of only watching from the sidelines. It gathers together tried, nonviolent, and lawful methods already experienced over the recent decades, in addition to offering a way of faithfully responding to God's word. It is not a theory that competes with just war or nonviolence/ pacifism, but it is a way to stop the vicious cycle of violence perpetuated by war.

To be the Christian church in the twenty-first century takes an unqualified commitment to following Jesus, and a respectful love of our fellow human beings. We tend to get caught up in the successes of our own kingdoms, believing that our own systems are the best, while resorting to inappropriate and disrespectful behavior toward those we consider our competitors or enemies. But the apostle Paul says that for those of us who allow our lives to be transformed by the Lord Jesus Christ, "our citizenship is in the heavens" (Philippians 3:20 PKC). That citizenship is not determined by national or ethnic boundaries.

Bibliography

Armstrong, Karen. "Compassion's Fruit," *AARP: The Magazine.* March/April 2005, 54-58.

Associated Press. "15 years ago minor-league catcher switched ball for potato in AA game." *Erie* (PA) *Times-News*, September 2, 2002, SportsWeek, 7.

Barclay, William. *The Lord's Prayer.* 1964, published as *The Plain Man Looks at the Lord's Prayer.* Reprint, Louisville, KY: Westminster John Knox Press, 1998.

Bauman, Clarence. *The Sermon on the Mount: The Modern Quest for Its Meaning.* Macon, GA: Mercer University Press, 1985.

Blackaby, Henry T., and Claude V. King. *Experiencing God.* Nashville: Broadman & Holman, 1994.

_____, and Melvin D. Blackaby. *Experiencing God Together: God's Plan to Touch Your World.* Nashville: Broadman & Holman, 2002.

Braght, Thieleman J. van. *The Bloody Theater or Martyrs Mirror of the Defenseless Christians.* Trans. Joseph F. Sohm from 1660 7th English ed. Scottdale, PA: Mennonite Publishing House, 1964.

Cho, Dan. "E-mail Study Corroborates Six Degrees of Separation." www.scientificamerican.com. *News*, August 8, 2003.

Coble, Ann Louise. *Cotton Patch for the Kingdom: Clarence Jordan's Demonstration Plot at Koinonia Farm.* Scottdale, PA, and Waterloo, ON: Herald Press, 2002.

Dale, Maryclaire. "Family of American beheaded in Iraq seeks answers." *The Lima* (Ohio) *News*, May 8, 2005, A3.

Davies, W. D., and Dale C. Allison Jr. *The Gospel According to Saint Matthew*, vol. 1 (*The International Critical Commentary*). Edinburgh: T&T Clark, 2000.

Davis, Ellen F., and Richard B. Hays. "Beyond criticism (Learning to read the Bible again)." *The Christian Century*. April 20, 2004, 26.

Dodd, C. H. *The Parables of the Kingdom*. Rev. Ed. First published 1935, James Nisbet and Company. Reprint, Great Britain: Fontana Books, 1961.

Epp, Albert H. *Discipleship Therapy: Healthy Christians, Healthy Churches*. Henderson, NE: Stairway Discipleship, 1993.

Ewald, George R. *Jesus and Divorce*. Scottdale, PA: Herald Press, 1991.

Fedarko, Kevin. "He Fights Terror with Books." *Parade Magazine*, April 6, 2003, 4ff.

Fischer, John. *12 Steps for the Recovering Pharisee (Like Me)*. Minneapolis: Bethany House, 2000.

Gardner, Richard B. *Matthew*. Believers Church Commentary Series. Scottdale, PA, and Waterloo, ON, 1991.

Getlin, Josh. "Decision invokes liberal West Coast image." *Erie* (PA) *Times-News*, June 28, 2002, 3.

Guthrie, Stan. "The Evangelical Scandal." *Christianity Today*, April 2005, 70.

Harrington, Daniel J., S.J. *The Gospel of Matthew*. Collegeville, MN: The Liturgical Press, 1991.

Hellwig, Monika K. *The Eucharist and the Hunger of the World*. New York: Paulist Press, 1976.

Holland, Linda. "My Money, My Life; The Online Angst of Full Disclosure." *New York Times*, January 14, 2001, final late edition, sec. 3.

Houser, Gordon. "Simply put, it's complex." *The Mennonite*, December 21, 2004, 30.

Hybels, Bill, and Rob Wilkins. *Descending into Greatness.* Grand Rapids, MI: Zondervan, 1993.

Jokinen, Beth L. "Grad gives back, honors counselor." *The Lima* (Ohio) *News*, June 15, 2006, B1.

Kates, Doug. "Rev. Bernice A. King says manners and civility are basis for a better world." *Corry* (PA) *Journal*, October 2, 2002, 12.

Kraybill, Donald B. *The Upside-Down Kingdom.* 25th anniversary edition. Scottdale, PA, and Waterloo, ON: Herald Press, 2003.

Kraybill, J. Nelson. "A Christian pledge of allegiance." *The Mennonite*, August 3, 2004, 8-11.

_____. "Apocalypse Now." *Christianity Today,* October 25, 1999, 30-40.

Kraybill, Ron. "Security in a world of terror?" *OurFaith*, Fall/Winter 2004, 8-9.

Lazarus, Edward. *Black Hills/White Justice: The Sioux Nation Versus the United States 1775 to the Present.* New York: HarperCollins, 1991.

Lewis, Monica. "Laws for everything from mustaches to monkeys." *Erie* (PA) *Times-News*, August 29, 2002, 11.

Long, Thomas G. *Hebrews: Interpretation, a Bible Commentary for Teaching and Preaching.* Louisville: John Knox Press, 1997.

Mennonite Church USA, *Confession of Faith in a Mennonite Perspective.* Scottdale, PA: Herald Press, 1995.

Mennonite Weekly Review staff. "Family forgives after hockey player's death." *Mennonite Weekly Review*, November 3, 2003, 1-2.

Neufeld, Thomas R. Yoder. *Ephesians.* Believers Church Bible Commentary Series. Waterloo, ON: Herald Press, 2002.

Olst, E. H. van. *The Bible and Liturgy.* Trans. John Vriend. Grand Rapids, MI: Eerdmans, 1991.

Ortberg, John. "Pharisees are us." *The Christian Century*, August 23, 2003, 20.

_____, Laurie Pederson, and Judson Poling. *Gifts: The Joy of Serving God*. Grand Rapids, MI: Zondervan, 2000.

Pitts, Leonard, Jr. *The Miami Herald*. "God not a GOP member." *The Lima* (Ohio) *News*, May 14, 2005, A6.

Preisker, H. "The Use of the Word Group *misthon*." *Theological Dictionary of the New Testament*, vol. 4. Ed. Gerhard Kittel, 1942. Trans. Geoffrey W. Bromiley. Grand Rapids, MI: Eerdmans, 1967, 1999.

Schrag, Paul. "Whirlwind of change." *Mennonite Weekly Review*, November 8, 2004, 1-2.

Sider, Ronald J. "Thinking biblically about politics." *Leader*, Spring 2005.

Stassen, Glen H., and David P. Gushee. *Kingdom Ethics: Following Jesus in Contemporary Context*. Downers Grove, IL: InterVarsity Press, 2003.

Stott, John R. W. *The Message of the Sermon on the Mount*. Downers Grove, IL: InterVarsity Press, 1978.

Jeb Bush et al v. Michael Schiavo. SC04-925. Supreme Court of Florida, 2004.

20/20, ABC News. Interview by Barbara Walters, April 17, 1992.

Wangerin, Walter Jr. *Miz Lil & the Chronicles of Grace*. San Francisco: Harper & Row, 1988.

Warren, Rick. *The Purpose-Driven Life*. Grand Rapids, MI: Zondervan, 2002.

Wiebe, Katie Funk. *Bless Me Too, My Father*. Scottdale, PA: Herald Press, 1988.

Willard, Dallas. *The Divine Conspiracy: Rediscovering Our Hidden Life in God*. New York: HarperSanFrancisco, 1998.

Wright, J. Edward. *The Early History of Heaven*. New York: Oxford University Press, 2000.

Yancey, Philip. *What's So Amazing About Grace?* Grand Rapids, MI: Zondervan, 1997.

Yoder, John Howard. *Body Politics: Five Practices of the*

Christian Community before the Watching World. Scottdale, PA: Herald Press, 2001.

_____. *The Politics of Jesus.* Grand Rapids, MI: Eerdmans, 1972.

Notes

Preface

1. John R. W. Stott, *The Message of the Sermon on the Mount* (Downers Grove, IL: InterVarsity Press, 1978), 15.

2. Stan Guthrie, "The Evangelical Scandal" (an interview of Ron Sider), *Christianity Today*, April 2005, 70.

3. Henry T. Blackaby and Melvin D. Blackaby, *Experiencing God Together: God's Plan to Touch Your World* (Nashville: Broadman & Holman, 2002), xi.

Chapter 1: Rules and Righteousness

1. David Wright, Copyright © 2004, used by permission. This personal story was written down by Wright at the request of the author.

2. Monica Lewis, "Laws for everything from mustaches to monkeys," *Erie* (PA) *Times-News*, August 29, 2002, 11.

3. Associated Press, "15 years ago minor-league catcher switched ball for potato in AA game," *Erie* (PA) *Times-News*, September 2, 2002, SportsWeek, 7.

4. Firman Gingerich, from a sermon at (Goshen) College Mennonite Church, Goshen, IN, October 6, 2002. Used by permission.

Chapter 2: Kingdom and Community

1. *Jeb Bush et al. v. Michael Schiavo*, SC04-925 (Florida Supreme Court, 2004).

2. Josh Getlin, "Decision invokes liberal West Coast image," *Erie* (PA) *Times-News*, June 28, 2002, 3.

3. Gordon Houser, "Simply put, it's complex," *The Mennonite*, December 21, 2004, 30.

4. Philip Yancey, *What's So Amazing About Grace?* (Grand Rapids, MI: Zondervan, 1997), 251.

5. Dallas Willard, *The Divine Conspiracy: Rediscovering Our Hidden Life in God* (San Francisco: HarperSanFrancisco, 1998), 67-8.

6. In Scripture quoted in this book, I have added brackets to give the plural of "heaven" where it appears in the Greek; for example, "kingdom of [the heavens]."

7. Thomas R. Yoder Neufeld, *Ephesians*, Believers Church Bible Commentary Series (Waterloo, ON: Herald Press, 2002), 168.

Chapter 3: Beatitudes and Blessings

1. Matthew 5—7, announcing the kingdom (Sermon on the Mount); 10, missionaries for the kingdom; 13, parables about the kingdom; 18, forgiveness in the kingdom; 24—25, consummation of the kingdom.

2. Richard B. Gardner, *Matthew*, Believers Church Bible Commentary Series (Scottdale, PA, and Waterloo, ON, 1991), 89.

3. C. H. Dodd, *The Parables of the Kingdom*, rev. ed. (1935; repr. Great Britain: Fontana Books, 1961), 36-7.

4. Dallas Willard, *The Divine Conspiracy: Rediscovering Our Hidden Life in God* (New York: HarperSanFrancisco, 1998), 106.

5. Monika K. Hellwig, *The Eucharist and the Hunger of the World* (New York: Paulist Press, 1976), 42-3.

6. Mennonite Church USA, *Confession of Faith in a Mennonite Perspective* (Scottdale, PA: Herald Press, 1995), from art. 24, "The Reign of God." Also available at http://www.mcusa-archives.org/library/resolutions/1995/index.html.

7. Fanny J. Crosby, *Gems of Praise*, 1873.

8. William P. Mackay, *New Praises of Jesus*, ca. 1867.

9. Donald B. Kraybill, *The Upside-Down Kingdom*, 25th

anniv. ed. (Scottdale, PA, and Waterloo, ON: Herald Press, 2003), 15-16.

10. John Howard Yoder, *Body Politics: Five Practices of the Christian Community before the Watching World* (Scottdale, PA: Herald Press, 2001), 47-70. See 1 Corinthians 12—14 as one biblical example.

11. Besides Matthew 5:12, see 5:46; 6:1, 2, 5, 16; and related verses 6:4, 6, 18.

Chapter 4: Law Is Law

1. This and the quotes in the following paragraph are from Associated Press services, *Erie* (PA) *Times-News*, December 8, 2003, 5.

2. Daniel J. Harrington, S.J., *The Gospel of Matthew* (Collegeville, MN: The Liturgical Press, 1991), 91.

3. John Fischer, *12 Steps for the Recovering Pharisee (Like Me)* (Minneapolis: Bethany House, 2000), 79.

4. Thomas G. Long, *Hebrews: Interpretation, a Bible Commentary for Teaching and Preaching* (Louisville: John Knox Press, 1997), 10.

5. Richard B. Gardner, *Matthew*, Believers Church Bible Commentary Series (Scottdale, PA, and Waterloo, ON, 1991), 105

6. George R. Ewald, *Jesus and Divorce* (Scottdale, PA: Herald Press, 1991), 58.

7. From wire service reports, *Erie* (PA) *Times-News*, June 8, 2004.

Chapter 5: Code of Conduct

1. Terry Waite, interview by Barbara Walters, *20/20*, April 17, 1992. Copyright © 2002 ABC Inc. All rights reserved.

2. Linda Holland, "My Money, My Life; The Online Angst of Full Disclosure," *New York Times*, January 14, 2001, final late edition, sec. 3.

3. Karen Armstrong, "Compassion's Fruit," *AARP: The Magazine*, March/April 2005, 54-58.

4. Thieleman J. van Braght, *The Bloody Theater or Martyrs Mirror of the Defenseless Christians*, trans. Joseph F. Sohm from 1660 7th English ed. (Scottdale, PA: Mennonite Publishing House, 1964), 741-2.

5. From a song by Linda M. Williams, First Church of the Brethren, San Diego; On Earth Peace, P. O. Box 188, New Windsor, Md. 21776.

6. In a story from *Miz Lil & the Chronicles of Grace* (San Francisco: Harper & Row, 1988, 25) Walter Wangerin Jr. tells how the phrase "spittin' image" derived from "spirit and image" as it was said in the American South: "*spee-it* and image."

7. Ken Blanchard and Don Shula, *Everyone's a Coach* (Grand Rapids, MI: Zondervan and Harper Business, 1995), 46.

Chapter 6: Minding the Mission

1. Robert H. Grant, "O worship the King," *Christian Psalmody*, 1833.

2. The earliest English translations starting around AD 1360 (Wycliffe) used the word *trespasses*, and this became used in worship. Even though the later King James Version used the terms *debts* and *debtors*, the tradition of *trespasses* has carried on through the generations.

3. The stories of Jesus' fourth discourse, Matthew 18, spell out the kingdom view of forgiveness. Greatness in the kingdom is based on humility, and humility is explained in terms of forgiveness.

4. Katie Funk Wiebe, *Bless Me Too, My Father* (Scottdale, PA: Herald Press, 1988), 59.

5. Staff, "Family forgives after hockey player's death," *Mennonite Weekly Review*, November 3, 2003, 1-2. From reports in *Canadian Mennonite*, *New York Times*, *Atlanta Journal-Constitution*, and *Toronto Star*.

6. E. H. van Olst, *The Bible and Liturgy*, trans. John Vriend (Grand Rapids, MI: Eerdmans, 1991), 16.

7. William Barclay, *The Lord's Prayer* (1964, *The Plain Man Looks at the Lord's Prayer*; repr., Louisville, KY: Westminster John Knox Press, 1998), 101-2.

8. Ibid., 107.

9. W. D. Davies and Dale C. Allison Jr., *The Gospel According to Saint Matthew*, vol. 1 (*The International Critical Commentary*) (Edinburgh: T&T Clark, 2000), 615.

10. NET, text-critical note to Matthew 6:13.

11. Wendell Berry, *Jayber Crow* (Washington, D.C.: Counterpoint, 2000), 51.

Chapter 7: Spiritual Secrets

1. John Ortberg, Laurie Pederson, Judson Poling, *Gifts: The Joy of Serving God* (Grand Rapids, MI: Zondervan, 2000), 84.

2. Beth L. Jokinen, "Grad gives back, honors counselor," *The Lima* (OH) *News*, June 15, 2006, B1.

3. H. Preisker, *Theological Dictionary of the New Testament*, ed. Gerhard Kittel, 1942, trans. Geoffrey W. Bromiley, vol. 4 (Grand Rapids, MI: Eerdmans, 1967, 1999), s.v. "The Use of the Word Group *misthon*," 699-700.

4. John Fischer, *12 Steps for the Recovering Pharisee (Like Me)* (Minneapolis: Bethany House, 2000), 158.

5. Rick Warren, *The Purpose-Driven Life* (Grand Rapids, MI: Zondervan, 2002), 17.

6. Henry T. Blackaby and Claude V. King, *Experiencing God* (Nashville: Broadman & Holman, 1994), 18.

Chapter 8: Material Matters

1. Ann Louise Coble, *Cotton Patch for the Kingdom: Clarence Jordan's Demonstration Plot at Koinonia Farm* (Scottdale, PA, and Waterloo, ON: Herald Press, 2002), 9-10.

2. Doug Kates, "Rev. Bernice A. King says manners and civility are basis for a better world," *Corry* (PA) *Journal*, October 2, 2002, 12, a report on King's October 1, 2002, lecture at Penn State-Erie, The Behrend College.

3. W. D. Davies and Dale C. Allison Jr., *The Gospel According to Saint Matthew*, vol. 1 (*The International Critical Commentary*) (Edinburgh: T&T Clark, 2000), 635-7.

4. Ron Kraybill, "Security in a world of terror?" *OurFaith*, Fall/Winter 2004, 8-9.

5. Everett J. Thomas, "Martial arts for making peace," *The Mennonite*, May 16, 2006, 16-17.

6. Bill Hybels and Rob Wilkins, *Descending into Greatness* (Grand Rapids, MI: Zondervan, 1993), 93.

7. Madeleine L'Engle, *Walking on Water: Reflections on Faith and Art* (Wheaton, IL: Harold Shaw Publishers, 1980), 31.

Chapter 9: Social Systems

1. Nick Berg Official Memorial Website, "Anecdotes," www.nickberg.org, 2006.

2. Maryclaire Dale, "Family of American beheaded in Iraq seeks answers," *The Lima* (OH) *News*, May 8, 2005, A3.

3. Leonard Pitts Jr., "God not a GOP member," *The Lima* (OH) *News*, May 14, 2005, A6.

4. Daniel J. Harrington, S.J., *The Gospel of Matthew* (Collegeville, MN: The Liturgical Press, 1991), 104-5.

5. Edward Lazarus, *Black Hills/White Justice: The Sioux Nation Versus the United States 1775 to the Present* (New York: HarperCollins, 1991).

6. Dallas Willard, *The Divine Conspiracy: Rediscovering Our Hidden Life in God* (New York: HarperSanFrancisco, 1998), 229.

7. Kevin Fedarko, "He Fights Terror with Books," *Parade Magazine*, April 6, 2003, 4ff. Further information can be found at www.ikat.org.

8. John Ortberg, "Pharisees are us," *The Christian Century*, August 23, 2003, 20.

9. Clarence Bauman, *The Sermon on the Mount: The Modern Quest for Its Meaning* (Macon, GA: Mercer University Press, 1985), 389.

Chapter 10: Fruits and Faithfulness

1. John Fischer, *12 Steps for the Recovering Pharisee (Like Me)* (Minneapolis: Bethany House, 2000), 58.

2. Albert H. Epp, *Discipleship Therapy: Healthy Christians, Healthy Churches* (Henderson, NE: Stairway Discipleship, 1993), 254.

Chapter 11: Call to Commitment

1. Mary A. Lathbury, "Break thou the bread of life," *Chautauqua Carols*, 1877.

2. Alice Parker, in the Fellowship class, Hawley, Massachusetts, May 14-23, 2002.

3. Alice Parker, unpublished manuscript.

4. Alice Parker, unpublished letter to the Fellowship class of May 14-23, 2002.

5. Dan Cho, "E-mail Study Corroborates Six Degrees of Separation," www.scientificamerican.com, August 8, 2003, News.

6. J. Nelson Kraybill, "Apocalypse Now," *Christianity Today*, October 25, 1999, 30-40.

7. J. Nelson Kraybill, "A Christian pledge of allegiance," *The Mennonite*, August 3, 2004, 8-11.

8. Ellen F. Davis and Richard B. Hays, "Beyond criticism (Learning to read the Bible again)," *Christian Century*, April 20, 2004, 26.

9. Clarence Bauman, *The Sermon on the Mount: The Modern Quest for Its Meaning* (Macon, GA: Mercer University Press, 1985), 423.

10. Paul Schrag, "Whirlwind of change," *Mennonite Weekly Review*, November 8, 2004, 1-2.

Appendix 2: Positions on Peace

1. John Howard Yoder, *The Politics of Jesus* (Grand Rapids, MI: Eerdmans, 1972), 193-214. The title of chapter 10 is "Let Every Soul Be Subject: Romans 13 and the Authority of the State."

2. Ibid., 207.

3. Ibid., 206.

4. Ibid., 212.

5. Ibid., 204.

6. Glen H. Stassen and David P. Gushee, *Kingdom Ethics: Following Jesus in Contemporary Context* (Downers Grove, IL: InterVarsity Press, 2003), 182, 213.

7. Ibid., 165.

8. Ibid., 164.

9. Ibid., 169.

10. Quotes in the preceding paragraphs are from Stassen and Gushee, *Kingdom Ethics*, 170-3.

The Author

Philip K. Clemens is pastor at Pike Mennonite Church in Elida, Ohio. He has served in the pastoral ministry at several churches since 1984. Before that he was professor of music at Goshen College from 1970 to 1986. He has taught music and served in music ministry since 1968. Clemens holds a doctorate in church music from Northwestern University, a master's in sacred music from Union Theological Seminary, and a bachelor's in divinity from Associated Mennonite Biblical Seminary. He has written numerous articles on music and pastoral ministry.